W0461422

Final Level Paper 14

Management Accounting: Information Strategy

First edition 2001

ISBN 0 7517 3517 5

British Library Cataloguing-in-Publication Data

A catalogue record for this book
is available from the British Library

Published by

BPP Publishing Limited
Aldine House, Aldine Place
London W12 8AW

www.bpp.com

Printed in Great Britain by Ashford Colour Press

If you use CIMA **Passcards**, you can be sure that the time you spend on final revision for your **2001 exams** is time well spent.

- They **save you time**: following the structure of the BPP Study Text for Paper 14, important facts on key exam topics are summarised for you
- They incorporate diagrams to kick start your memory
- They are pocket-sized: you can run through them **anytime** and **anywhere**
- CIMA **Passcards** focus on the exam you will be facing
- They provide you with suggestions on subject examinability in **exam focus points**

Run through the complete set of **Passcards** as often as you can during your final revision period. The day before the exam, try to go through the **Passcards** again. You will then be well on your way to passing your exams. **Good luck!**

Contents

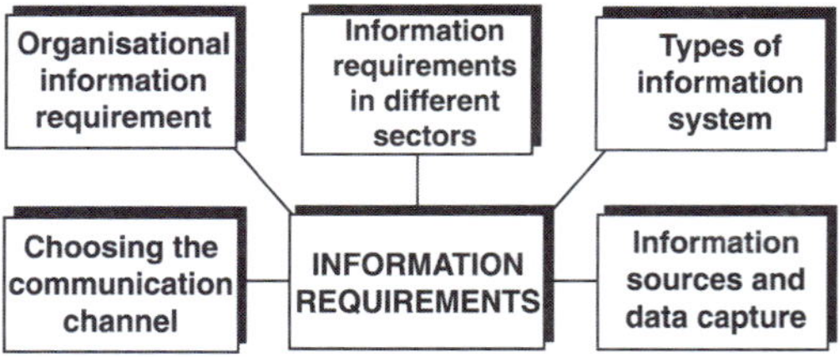

Organisational information requirements

Data is the raw material for data processing. Data consists of numbers, letters and symbols and relates to facts, events, and transactions.

Information is data that has been processed in such a way as to be meaningful to the person who receives it.

Organisations require information for a range of purposes:

- Planning
- Controlling
- Recording transactions
- Performance measurement
- Decision making

Planning requires a knowledge of the available resources, possible time-scales and the likely outcome under alternative scenarios.

Control information is required to assess whether progress is proceeding as planned, or if it is necessary to take some form of corrective action.

Information recording *transaction details* is required. Reasons include:

- Evidence in a case of dispute
- Legal requirement
- Management purposes

Information that facilitates *performance measurement* enables comparisons against budget, plan, other departments, other organisations.

Decision making

Decision making can be analysed into three *levels* - strategic, tactical and operational.

Strategic information is used to plan the objectives of the organisation.

Strategic information is

- Derived from internal and external sources
- Summarised at a high level
- Relevant to the long term
- Concerned with the whole organisation
- Often prepared on 'ad hoc' basis
- Quantitative and qualitative
- Uncertain, as the future can not be predicted

Tactical information is used in decisions involving how resources are obtained and used to achieving objectives. Tactical information is:

- Primarily generated internally (but may have a limited external component)
- Summarised at a lower level
- Relevant to the short and medium term

- Concerned with activities or departments
- Prepared routinely and regularly
- Based on quantitative measures

Operational information is used to ensure that specific tasks are planned and carried out.

Operational information is

- Derived from internal sources
- Detailed
- Immediate/short term
- Task-specific
- Prepared frequently, routinely
- Largely quantitative

The qualities of good information Pilot paper

Identifying weaknesses

Bad information *lacks* certain desirable characteristics. Faults may be intrinsic in the information itself or they may arise because of the method of presentation.

- It is not *relevant* to the user
- It is not *complete*
- It is not *accurate* or its level of accuracy is inappropriate
- It lacks *clarity*
- It does not inspire *confidence* in the user
- It is not appropriately *communicated*

- The *volume* is wrong (eg information overload)
- It is not *timely* (too early or, more often, too late)
- The *cost* of providing it exceeds its value

ACCURATE

You may like a mnemonic which roughly corresponds with the above list.

A ccurate

C omplete

C ost-beneficial

U ser-targeted

R elevant

A uthoritative (in terms of source)

T imely

E asy to use

Three C's can be added to the mnemonic.

C oncise

C hannel (of communication)

C larity (of presentation)

> *Exam focus.* It is essential that you relate your knowledge of information theory to the question.

Information requirements in different sectors

Manufacturing sector – examples of strategic information

- Future demand estimates
- New product development plans
- Competitor analysis

Manufacturing sector – examples of tactical information

- Variance analysis
- Departmental accounts
- Stock turnover

Manufacturing sector – examples of operational information

- Production reject rate
- Materials and labour used
- Stock levels

Service sector – examples of strategic information

- Forecast sales growth and market share
- Profitability, capital structure

Service sector – examples of tactical information

- Resource utilisation such as average staff time charged out, number of customers per hairdresser etc
- Customer satisfaction rating

Service sector – examples of operational information

- Staff timesheets
- Customer waiting time
- Individual customer feedback

Public sector – examples of strategic information

- Population demographics
- Expected government policy

Public sector – examples of tactical information

- Hospital occupancy rates
- Average class sizes
- Percent of reported crimes solved

Public sector – examples of operational information

- Staff timesheets
- Student daily attendance records
- Hospital beds available

Non-profit and charities – examples of strategic information

- Activities of other charities
- Government (and in some cases overseas government) policy
- Public attitudes

Non-profit and charities – examples of tactical information

- Percent of revenue spent on admin
- Average donation
- Customer' satisfaction statistics

Non-profit and charities – examples of operational information

- Households collected from
- Banking documentation
- Donation slips

Types of information system

Types of information system

Transaction processing systems, or data processing systems, are the lowest level in an organisation's use of information systems. They are used for routine transactions processing.

A **management information system** (MIS) converts data from internal and external sources into information, and communicates that information in an appropriate form to managers at all levels.

The following table shows the typical inputs, processes and outputs at each level of a Management Information System.

	Inputs	*Processes*	*Outputs*
Strategic	Plans Competitor information Market information	Summarise Investigate Compare Forecast	Key ratios Ad hoc market analysis Strategic plans
Tactical	Historical data Budget data	Compare Classify Summarise	Variance analyses Exception reports
Operational	Customer orders Programmed stock control levels	Update files Output reports	Updated files Listings Invoices

Decision support systems are used by management to assist in making decisions on issues which are unstructured and have high levels of uncertainty.

DSS can describe a range of systems, from fairly simple information models based on spreadsheets to expert systems.

An **executive information system** (EIS) is a type of DSS which gives the senior executive easy access to key internal and external data'.

The differences between a Management Information System (MIS) and an Executive Information System (EIS) are outlined in the following table.

MIS	*EIS*
Many traditional information systems imitate the layout of **manual daybooks**, so that the user has to scroll through lists of individual transactions in order to find a period or category total.	An EIS starts at the summary, and then permits, but does not force, the executive to **drill down** to lower levels.
In traditional MIS, **exception reporting** is likely to be a strong feature. For example, if Department E is 20% off budget in a period, this will be highlighted, so that the manager can take appropriate action.	In an EIS, the user may be equally interested in Department D, which was exactly on budget. The EIS is less likely to discriminate in this way.
Many MIS are only designed to provide information that has been generated **within** the organisation.	An EIS is usually designed to allow **internal and external** information to be reported, although in practice the less structured and predictable nature of much external information may make this difficult.

Expert systems are a form of DSS that allow users to benefit from expert knowledge and information. The system will consist of a database holding specialised data and rules about what to do in, or how to interpret, a given set of circumstances.

Business applications of expert systems include:

- Legal advice
- Credit scoring
- Tax advice
- Forecasting
- Surveillance, for example of machines in a factory, to determine when they need maintenance
- Diagnostic systems
- Project management

The components of an expert system are shown on the following diagram.

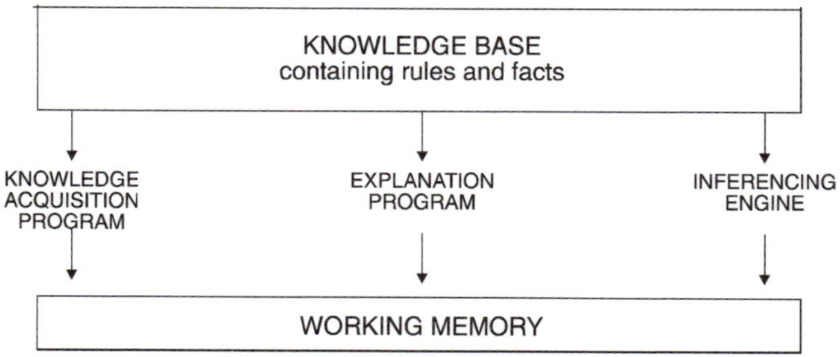

Advantages of expert systems include:

- Information and knowledge is permanently recorded
- The knowledge is easily duplicated
- They are consistent
- They can be documented
- They are fast

Limitations of expert systems include:

- They can be expensive
- The technology is still in its infancy in many areas
- A new system in the first place will need extensive testing
- People are naturally more creative
- Systems have a very narrow focus
- Managers may be reluctant to follow the advice

Information sources and data capture

Internal data/information sources include the following:

- Transactions data
- Accounting records
- The 'grapevine'
- Formal communications

External data sources such as the following will also be used

- Customers
- Publications (newspapers, technical journals)
- Central and local government
- Consultancies

- Other organisations eg EDI, extranet
- On-line services

Efficient data collection

To produce meaningful information it is first necessary to capture the underlying data. Common data collection methods include:

- Optical Character Recognition (OCR) - used with scanners
- MICR
- Bar coding and EPOS devices
- Optical mark reading (OMR)
- EFTPOS
- Smart cards
- Interactive websites
- EDI
- Voice recognition

Choosing the communication channel *Pilot paper*

A channel that will help the receiver correctly interpret the information should be chosen.

The choice of medium will depend upon numerous factors, including the following.

- Time
- Complexity
- Distance

- Written record
- Interaction
- Degree of confidentiality
- The recipient
- Cost

The features and limitations of common communication tools are outlined in the following table.

Tool	Features / Advantages	Limitations
Conversation	Usually unstructured so can discuss a wide range of topics Requires little or no planning Gives a real impression of feelings	Temptation to lose focus May be easily forgotten
Meeting	Allows multiple opinions to be expressed Can discuss and resolve a wide range of issues	Can highlight differences and conflict if not managed efficiently. 'Louder' personalities may dominate proceedings Costly in terms of personnel time A focused agenda and an effective Chair should prevent these limitations hindering the meeting

Tool	Features/Advantages	Limitations
Presentation	Complex ideas can be communicated Visual aids such as slides can help the communication process The best presentations will leave a lasting impression	Requires planning and skill Poorly researched or presented material can lead to audience resentment Also see Chapter 3
Memorandum	Provides a permanent record of an internal message Adds formality to internal communications	If used too often or the message is too general people may ignore it Can come across as impersonal
Letter	Provides a permanent record of an external message Adds formality Use a clear, simple structure, for example • Letterhead • Reference or heading • Date • Recipient name and address • Greeting/ salutation • Subject • Substance • Close	If inaccurate or poorly presented provides a permanent record of incompetence May be slow to arrive depending on distance and the postal service

Tool	Features/Advantages	Limitations
Report	Provides a permanent, often comprehensive written record Use a clear, simple structure. There is no one correct format. An example that could be adapted to suit the report requirements is… • Meaningful Title • Author name and position • Purpose /Terms of Reference • Procedure followed • Findings • Conclusion / Recommendations Where necessary use a hierarchy of headings to aid clarity. For example… • 1 Section heading • (a) sub heading • (i) sub point	Complex messages may be misunderstood in the absence of immediate feedback Reports that reach (necessarily) negative conclusions can lead to negative impressions of the author

Tool	Features/Advantages	Limitations
Telephone	Good when you do not require (or you would prefer not to have) a permanent written record Can provide some of the 'personal touch' to people in geographically remote locations Conference calls allow multiple participants	Receiver may not be available; 'phone-tag' is a frustrating pass-time! (Voice-mail may help) Can be disruptive to receiver if in the middle of another task No written record gives greater opportunity for misunderstandings
Facsimile	Enables reports and messages to reach remote locations quickly	Easily seen by others Fax machine may not be cleared Complex images do not transmit well
Electronic mail	Provides a written record Attachments (eg Reports) can be included Quick Automated 'Read receipts' mean you know if the message has been received Can be sent to multiple recipients easily, can be forwarded on to others	Requires some computer literacy to use effectively People may not check their e-mail regularly Lack of privacy – can be forwarded easily Long messages may best be dealt with via other means, or as attachments

Tool	Features/Advantages	Limitations
Video-conference	This is in effect a meeting conducted using a computer and video system Provides more of a personal touch than the telephone, but less than a 'physical' meeting Some non-verbal messages (eg gestures) will be received	The hardware is expensive compared to telephone May be dominated by the most confident participant(s) Cross-border cultural differences may be unintentionally ignored as participants feel 'at home' Image quality is often poor – resulting in not much more than an expensive telephone conference call!

Exam focus. The pilot paper included a question regarding how certain characteristics of information can help the recipient's understanding.

Remember that both the content of the message and the communication channel used influence the communication process.

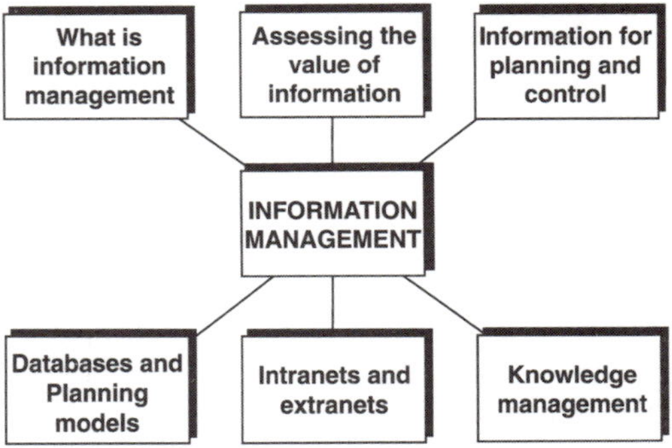

What is information management?

Information management entails the following tasks.

- Identifying current and future information needs
- Identifying information sources
- Collecting the information
- Storing the information
- Facilitating existing methods of using information and identifying new ways of using it
- Ensuring that information is communicated to those who need it
- Ensuring information is not available to those who are not entitled to see it

Technology has provided new sources of information, new ways of collecting it, storing it and processing it, and new methods of communicating and sharing it.

Assessing the value of information

Factors that make information a valuable commodity

Information is now recognised as a valuable resource, and a key tool in the quest for a competitive advantage.

Unlike certain commodities the value of information in general is not based on scarcity: indeed the most frequent complaint of many modern managers is that there is far too much of it about.

The value of obtaining information

The **cost** of collecting information bears no relation to its **value**. An item of information that leads to an increase in profit of £90 is not worth having if it costs £100 to collect. Information that is obtained but not used brings no benefit.

While nobody doubts that information is vital, it is not always easy to construct an economic assessment of the value of information, as the **financial consequences** of a decision are not always easy to predict or to **measure**.

Traditional **investment appraisal methods** (eg the payback method, the accounting rate of return and discounted cashflow methods) can be applied with varying degrees of success to problems of this kind.

The benefits of a proposed information system

- Savings generated because the old system will no longer be operated
- Extra savings or revenue benefits because of the improvements or enhancements

- Some benefits might be **intangible**, or impossible to give a money value to – they should still be identified and fully explained. Examples include:
  - Greater customer satisfaction
  - Improved staff morale
  - Better decision making

Information for planning and control

Strategic planning, management control and operational control may be seen as a **hierarchy** of planning and control decisions. (This is sometimes called the *Anthony hierarchy*).

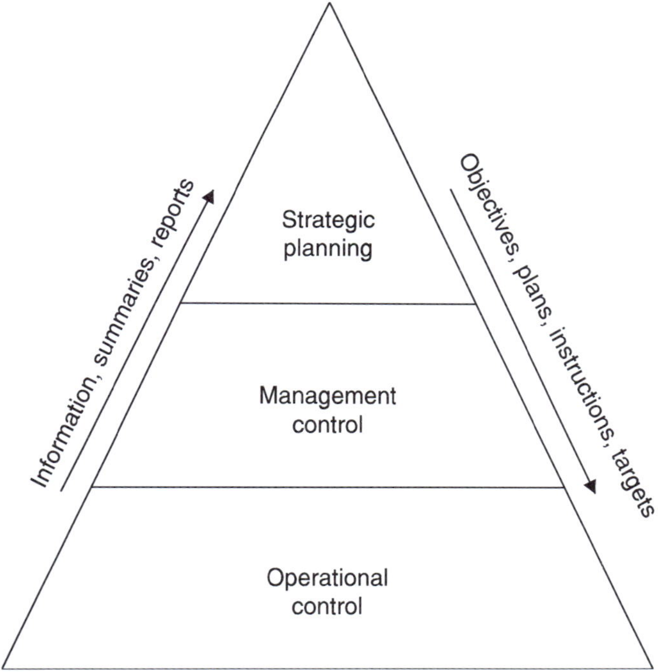

Strategic planning is a process of deciding on objectives of the organisation, on changes in these objectives, on the resources used to attain these objectives and on the policies that are to govern the acquisition, use and disposition of these resources.

Tactical planning/control (also called management control) means ensuring that resources are obtained and used effectively and efficiently in the accomplishment of the organisation's objectives.

Operational control ensures that specific tasks are carried out effectively and efficiently. It focuses on individual tasks, and is carried out within the strictly defined guidelines issued by strategic planning and tactical control decisions.

Examples of **unstructured** and **structured** decisions at the different levels of management are given below.

Decision level	Structured	Semi-structured	Unstructured
Operational	Stock control procedures	Selection of new supplier	Hiring supervisor
Tactical	Selection of products to discount	Allocation of budget	Expanding into a new design
Strategic	Major investment decisions	Entry to new market; new product line	Reorganisation of whole company

Decisions must be taken in response to choices and options regarding how the organisation responds to the environment, and how its internal activities are to be run.

The decision making process

The stages in making a decision are as follows.

Step 1 Problem **recognition**

Step 2 Problem **definition** and structuring

Step 3 Identifying **alternative courses of action**

Step 4 Making and **communicating** the decision

Step 5 **Implementation** of the decision

Step 6 **Monitoring** the effects of the decision

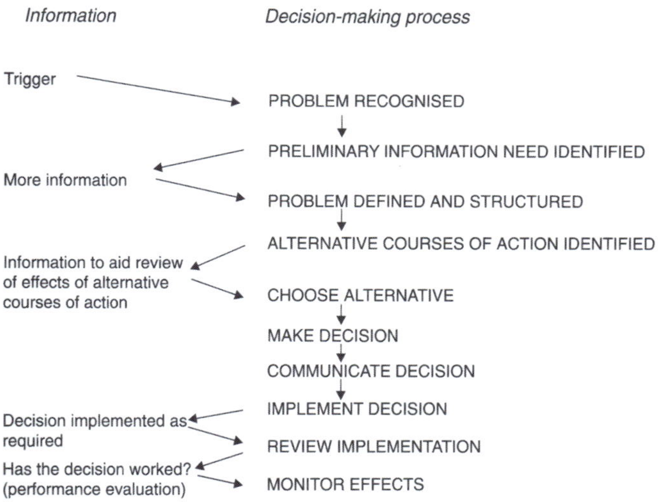

Risk and uncertainty in decision-making

Risk involves events which may or may not occur, but whose probability of occurrence can be calculated statistically.

Uncertainty involves situations or events whose outcome cannot be predicted with statistical confidence.

Bringing risk and uncertainty into the decision-making process

- Conservative estimates
- Looking at the worst possible and best possible outcomes
- Sensitivity analysis
- Assessing probabilities and calculating the expected value of costs or benefits

Perfect and imperfect information

- **Perfect** information is information which will predict the future with absolute **certainty**
- **Imperfect** information is information, which cannot be guaranteed to be completely accurate. Almost all information is therefore imperfect - but may still be very useful

Critical success factors

Using CSFs

The use of CSFs can help determine the information requirements of management and this in turn assists in identifying what information systems are required.

- For each executive, critical success factors are the few key areas of the job where things must go right for the organisation to flourish
- Usually there are fewer than ten of these factors that any one executive should monitor
- CSFs are very time dependent, so they should be examined as often as necessary to keep abreast of the current business climate

Sources of CSFs

Rockart suggests four sources of CSFs.

- The industry that the business is in
- The company itself and its situation in the industry
- The environment
  - Consumer trends
  - Economy
  - Political factors
- Temporal organisational factors (areas of corporate activity which are currently unacceptable)

Performance indicators

One approach to defining CSFs is to ask personnel to:

- List the organisation's corporate objectives
- Determine those factors which are critical to accomplishing objectives
- Determine a small number of prime measures for each factor
  - Determining prime measures is not always straightforward
  - Where quantitative data is used, there are several possible approaches
    - Physical quantities
    - Monetary values
    - Ratios

Knowledge management

Knowledge is:

- Information within people's minds

- Now commonly viewed as a sustainable source of competitive advantage
- Of no value unless it is applied to decisions and actions in a purposeful business context
- Locked up in people's heads unless they choose to share it

Knowledge management programmes are attempts at:

- Designing and installing techniques and processes to create, protect and use explicit knowledge (that is knowledge that the company knows that it has)
- Designing and creating environments and activities to discover and release tacit knowledge (that is, knowledge that the company does not know it has).

There are many **approaches to KM** including:

- Document management
- Information management
- Business intelligence
- Competence management
- Information systems management
- Intellectual asset management
- Innovation, business process design, and so on

KM has **two distinctive tasks**:

- To facilitate the creation of knowledge
- To manage the way people share and apply it

Companies that prosper with KM will be those that realise that it is as much about managing people as about information and technology.

Systems that aid KM

Computer Supported Co-operative Working, or 'collaborative' working, is a term which combines the understanding of the way people work in groups with the enabling technologies of computer networking and associated hardware, software, services and techniques.

Organisations rely upon people working together so information systems should be designed to help people to do this. This is the principle behind Computer Supported Co-operative Working (CSCW).

Groupware is a term used to describe a collection of IT tools designed for the use of co-operative or collaborative work groups. Groupware can involve software, hardware, services, and/or group process support.

It is when groupware is used to share information with colleagues that it comes into its own. Features include the following.

- A scheduler
- A contacts list
- 'To do' lists
- A jotter
- Messaging, comprising e-mail and routing facilities
- Access to an information database and customisable 'views' of the information
- Group scheduling

- Public folders
- Conferencing (participation in public online discussions)
- Assigning tasks
- Voting
- Hyperlinks in mail messages
- Workflow management (see below)

Workflow

Workflow is a term used to describe the defined series of tasks within an organisation to produce a final outcome.

Sophisticated workgroup computing applications allow the user to define different workflows for different types of jobs. There are three common types.

- Image-based workflow systems are designed to automate the flow of paper through an organisation, by transferring the paper to digital 'images'
- Form-based workflow systems are designed to route forms intelligently throughout an organisation. These forms, unlike images, are text-based and consist of editable fields

Intranets and extranets

Intranets

An **intranet** is an **internal** network used to share information. Intranets utilise **Internet technology** and protocols.

The main cost of an intranet is the staff time required to set up and maintain the system.

The **benefits** of an intranet:

- Savings from the elimination of storage, printing and distribution of documents
- Documents on-line are often more widely used
- It is easier to update information in electronic form
- Wider access to corporate information should open the way to more flexible working patterns

Extranets

An **extranet** is an intranet that is accessible to **authorised outsiders**.

Whereas an intranet resides behind a firewall and is accessible only to people who are members of the same company or organisation, an extranet provides various levels of accessibility to outsiders.

Extranets are becoming a very popular means for **business partners** to exchange information. They facilitate better use of knowledge held within an organisation - by facilitating access to that knowledge.

Databases and planning models

The way in which data is held on a system affects the ease by which the data can be accessed and manipulated.

Many modern software packages are **built around a database** – a comprehensive set of data for a number of different users.

Advantages of a database system:

- Avoidance of duplication of data

- Data is looked upon as serving the organisation as a whole
- Encourages management to analyse data
- Data on file is independent of the user programs that access the data, allowing greater flexibility
- Developing new application programs with a database system is easier

Exam focus. Databases and planning models could be examined in the context of knowledge management and for data warehousing and data mining (covered in Chapter 4).

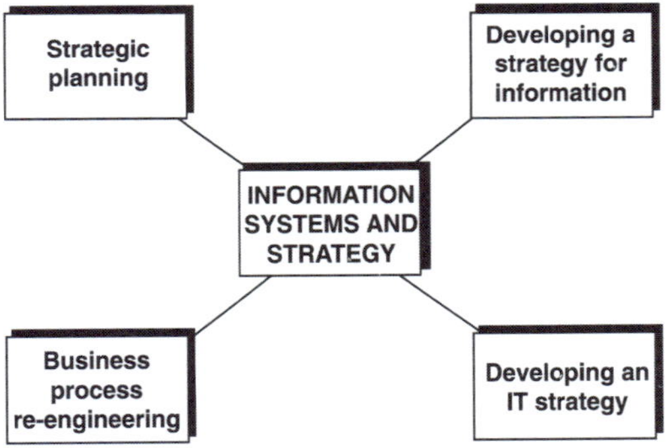

Strategic planning

Strategic planning is a complex process. It involves taking a view of both the organisation, and the future that it is likely to encounter, and then attempting to organise the structure and resources of the organisation accordingly.

Strategy can be defined as 'A course of action, including the specification of resources required, to achieve a specific objective.'

Strategic planning is the formulation, evaluation and selection of strategies for the purpose of preparing a long-term plan of action to attain objectives. *(CIMA, Official Terminology)*

The strategic planning process is summarised in the following diagram.

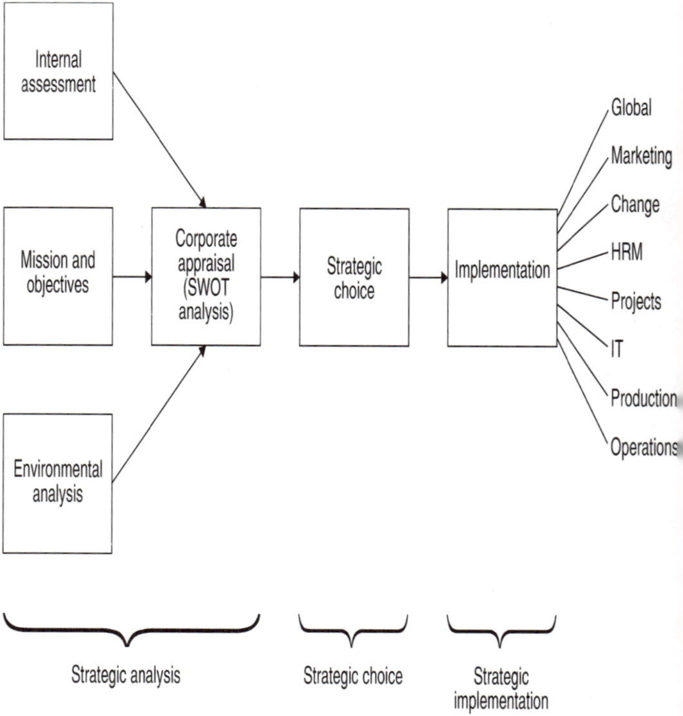
Internal assessment
Mission and objectives
Environmental analysis
Corporate appraisal (SWOT analysis)
Strategic choice
Implementation
Global
Marketing
Change
HRM
Projects
IT
Production
Operations
Strategic analysis
Strategic choice
Strategic implementation

Measuring strategic planning effectiveness

An important role of both the finance and information technology functions is to help ensure the agreed strategy is proceeding according to plan. The table below outlines the rationale behind this view.

Measuring strategic planning effectiveness (US Institute of Management Accountants (IMA))

	Traditional view	Strategic implications
Cost	The finance and information technology functions can be relatively expensive	Shared services and outsourcing could be used to capture cost savings
IT	IT has traditionally been transaction based	IT/IS should be integrated with business strategy
Value	The finance and IT functions do not add value	Redesign the functions
Strategy	Accountants and IT managers are seen as scorekeepers and administrators rather than as a business partner during the strategic planning process	Change from cost-orientated to market-orientated ie development of more effective strategic planning systems

Developing a strategy for information

Pilot paper

Vision and reality

A company that has a vision of its own future, and some idea of how information technology can be used to turn that vision into reality, may be able to use new technologies for strategic advantage.

One approach to **creating a vision** is to adopt a familiar three step approach, involving answering three questions about the organisation.

- Where are we now?

This question can be answered using standard techniques such as a strengths, weaknesses, opportunities, threats (SWOT) analysis.

- Where do we want to be?

This does not have to be a continuation in the organisation's current direction. It must be challenging, attainable and communicated to those who will implement it.

- How will we get there?

Once the first two questions have been answered, the **strategy** (in answer to the third question) can be defined.

A second approach takes the view that insiders are too tied to 'the way we do things now', and recommends the involvement of **outsiders**.

Information and competitive advantage

Formal management strategies and plans for information can be grouped together under the term **Information Management (IM).**

Information management involves the use of manual and computerised Information Systems (IS).

An information strategy for an organisation can be said to cover three areas: **systems**, **technology** and **management**.

The **information systems (IS) strategy** has been defined as the long-term directional plan; seen to be business-led, demand-oriented and concerned to exploit IT either to support business strategies or create new strategic options.

The **information technology (IT) strategy** leads on from the IS strategy. It deals with the technologies of:

- Computing
- Communications
- Data
- Application systems

This provides a framework for the analysis and design of the technological infrastructure of an organisation.

The information management (IM) strategy refers to the basic approach an organisation has to the management of its information systems, including:

- Planning IS/IT developments
- Organisational environment of IS
- Control (eg cost control)
- Technology (eg systems development methodologies)

Why have an IT strategy?

- IT involves high costs
- IT is critical to the success of many organisations
- IT is now used as part of the commercial strategy in the battle for competitive advantage
- IT is required by the economic context (from a macro-economic point of view)

- IT affects all levels of management
- IT affects the way management information is created and presented
- IT requires effective management to obtain the maximum benefit
- IT involves many stakeholders within and outside the organisation
- IT is a high cost activity

The importance of technology

Any strategic view of IT must take technical issues into account. Ignoring the technology-based choices in IT is rather like ignoring interest rates when you are borrowing money.

Technological change can affect the activities of organisations as follows.

- The type of products or services that are made and sold
- The way in which products are made
- The way in which services are provided
- The way in which markets are identified
- The way in which employees are mobilised

The **benefits of technological change** could include:

- Reduced production costs
- Better quality products and services
- The development of products and services that did not exist before

- Products or services provided more quickly or effectively
- Free staff from repetitive work

The importance of management

It is argued that success or failure in implementing IT is a result not so much of the systems themselves but the management effort behind them.

Developing an IT strategy

An IT strategy must deal with three issues.

- The organisation's overall business needs
- The organisation's current use of IT
- The potential opportunities and threats that IT can bring

Each of these three issues involves different personnel, and requires a slightly different approach. A diagrammatic representation of IT strategy development follows.

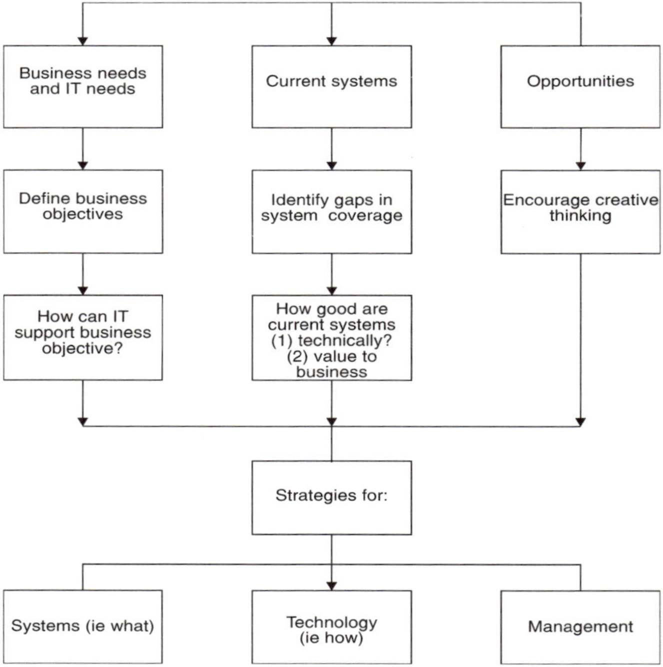

Identifying business needs

There are a number of techniques for identifying business needs. One such technique is the use of critical success factors (CSFs) which we described in Chapter 2. The CSF approach to IS/IT planning is illustrated in the following diagram.

The critical success factor approach to IS/IT

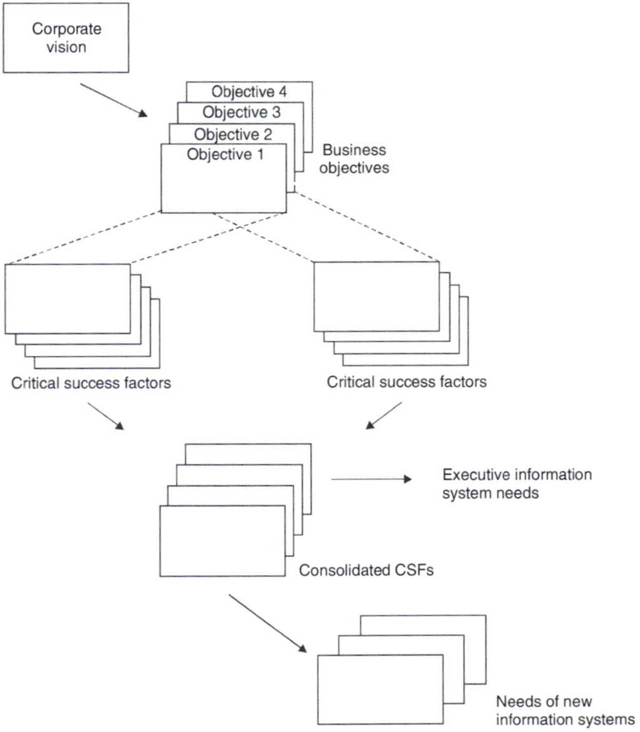

Source: IT Strategy for Business, Joe Peppard Chapter 4, Garret Hickey

Evaluating current systems

Systems specialists and providers indicate the system's technical quality in terms of:

- Reliability
- Ease of maintenance
- Cost efficiency

Users can rate a system on its:

- Business impact (eg how would we manage without it?)
- Ease of use and user-friendliness
- Frequency of use (indicates its importance and value)

Users may suggest evolutionary add-ons to systems.

Earl suggests a grid to analyse an organisation's use of information systems.

		Technical Quality	
		Low	*High*
Business Value	*Low*	Divest (dispose of)	Reassess
	High	Renew, enhance	Maintain, enhance

IT can be said to function in four different ways in an organisation. **McFarlan** analysed this in a grid, as follows.

		Strategic impact of applications development portfolio (ie future systems)	
		Low	*High*
Strategic impact of existing systems	*Low*	Support	High potential
	High	Key operational	Strategic

IT has a **support** role for a business where information systems have little relevance to a firm's existing or future success. This means that:

- IT requires below average investment
- IT requires little management attention

If existing IT applications are important but future IT developments are not anticipated to impact greatly, it has what is termed a **key operational** role (or factory role).

IT has a **strategic** role where existing and future developments are at the heart of the company's future success. In fact, the business operation depends on IT.

IT's **high potential** role (or turnaround role) is where existing IT is not important, but future developments are likely to have a significant impact.

A company is not condemned to occupying one square on the grid forever.

Opportunities and threats

Opportunities cannot always be identified from the processes described above. Instead, creative thinking in the organisation should be encouraged.

There are three ways in which creative thinking and opportunity 'spotting' can be encouraged.

- Techniques to foster innovation, such as think tanks, brainstorming sessions
- Consulting (or recruiting) outsiders
- Using technology to change working practices

The inputs and outputs of the IS/IT strategic planning process are summarised on the following diagram.

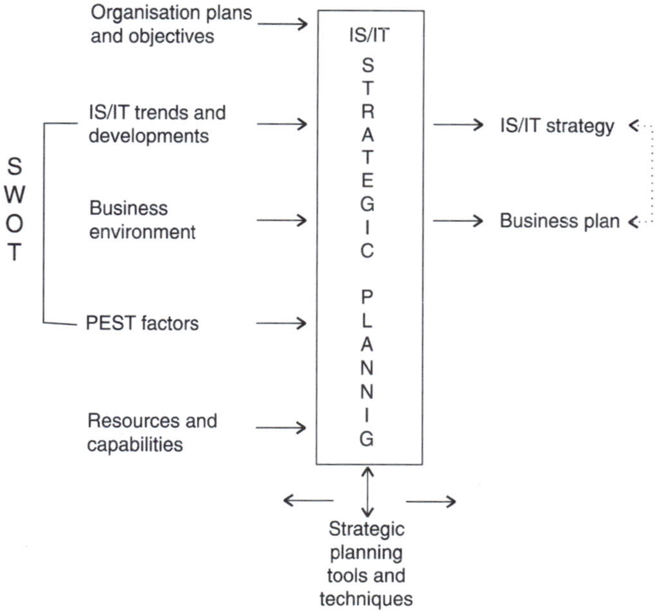

Business process re-engineering (BPR)

Business Process Re-engineering is the fundamental rethinking and radical redesign of business processes to achieve dramatic improvements in critical contemporary measures of performance, such as cost, quality, service and speed. *(Hammer and Champy)*

BPR can lead to fundamental changes in the way an organisation functions.

Principles of BPR

Hammer presents seven principles for BPR.

- Processes should be designed to achieve a desired outcome rather than focusing on existing tasks
- Personnel who use the output from a process should perform the process
- Information processing should be included in the work which produces the information
- Geographically dispersed resources should be treated as if they are centralised
- Parallel activities should be linked rather than integrated
- 'Doers' should be allowed to be self-managing
- Information should be captured once, at source

Davenport and Short prescribe a **five-step approach to BPR**.

Step 1. Develop the business vision and process objectives. BPR is driven by a business vision, which implies specific business objectives such as cost reduction, time reduction, output quality improvement, and empowerment.

Step 2. Identify the processes to be redesigned.

Step 3. Understand and measure the existing processes - so old mistakes are not repeated and to provide a baseline for future improvements.

Step 4. Identify IT levers. Awareness of IT capabilities can and should influence process design.

Step 5. Design and build a prototype of the new process. The actual design should not be viewed as the end of the BPR process - it should be viewed as a prototype, with successive alterations. The use of a prototype enables the involvement of customers.

IT and BPR

Simply throwing IT at a problem does not cause it to be re-engineered. For technology to deliver value, it must help enact the processes that satisfy business requirements.

'It is the disruptive power of technology, its ability to break the rules that limit how we conduct our work, that makes it critical to companies looking for competitive advantage.'

(Hammer and Champy)

Why focus on processes?

To properly harness the resources within a business a clear agreement of the management and implementation of processes is needed. Without this focus on processes:

- It is unclear how value is achieved or can continue to be achieved
- The affects of change on the operation of the business is hard to predict
- There is no basis to achieve business improvement in a consistent way
- Knowledge is lost as people move around or out of the business
- Cross-functional interaction is not encouraged
- It is difficult to align the strategy of an organisation with its people, systems and resources

Problems with BPR

- BPR has become allied in managers minds with narrow targets such as reductions in staff numbers and cost-cutting measures

- Managers tend to focus on narrow aspects of the organisation
- It is argued that process re-engineering does not take the wider picture into account

> *Exam focus.* Business process re-engineering may be referred to simply as process engineering. The principles outlined here could also be applied to questions regarding efficiency and workflow.

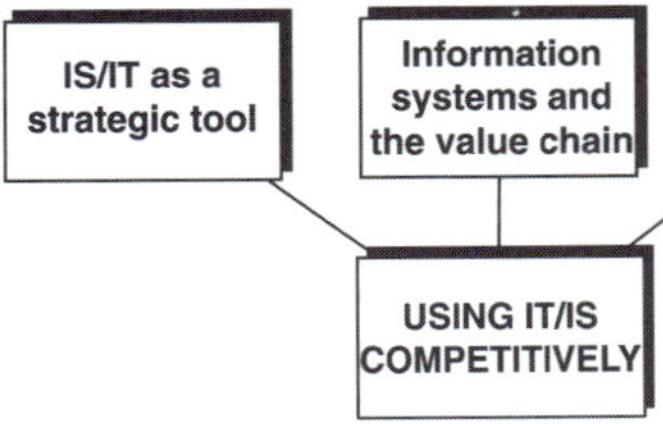

Using IS/IT as a strategic tool

Pilot paper

Information Systems (IS) and Information Technology (IT) can be used as a source of competitive advantage.

Competitive advantage is a profitable and sustainable position.

IT has the potential to change the nature of competition within an industry in three ways. IT can:

- Change the industry structure
- Create new businesses and industries
- Be used to create competitive advantage

Changing the industry structure

Pilot paper

Porter identified **five competitive forces** operating in a competitive environment.

1. The threat of new entrants

Defensively, IT can increase economies of scale, raise the capital cost of entry (by requiring a similar investment in IT) or by tying customers and suppliers into the supply/distribution chain.

Offensively, IT can leap over entry barriers. An example is the use of Internet banking, which sometimes obviates the need to establish a branch network.

2. The bargaining power of suppliers

The bargaining power of suppliers can be eroded by IT in three ways.

- By increasing competition between suppliers - IT can facilitate easy scanning of prices from a number of suppliers
- Suppliers' power can be shared - an example is using CAD to design components
- Suppliers can be integrated, in purely administrative terms, by a system of electronic data interchange

3. The bargaining power of customers

- IT can be used to 'lock customers in'
- IT can raise switching costs – for example where IT provides a distribution channel for certain services (eg airline tickets)
- Customer information systems can facilitate the identification of customer needs

4. The threat of substitute products/services

- IT is the basis for new leisure activities
- IT can add value to existing services by allowing more detailed analysis, by generating cost advantages, or by extending the market

5. The existing competitive rivalry in the industry

- IT can be used to compete – as a source of competitive advantage (this is covered later)

- Alternatively, IT can be used as a collaborative venture, perhaps to set up new communications networks eg Electronic Data Interchange (EDI), Value Added Network Services (VANS) and extranets
- IT can create new businesses - for example, the Internet Service Provider industry
- The publishing industry provides a good example of an existing industry affected by IS/IT. Encyclopaedia publishers such as Encyclopaedia Britannica have moved from paper-based products to a hybrid CD-ROM \ web-based product
- The nature of competitors can also be influenced - Encyclopaedia Britannica now has to compete not only against traditional encyclopaedia producers, but also against software companies such as Microsoft (with Microsoft Encarta)

Criticisms of Porter's five forces model

- The model relies on a static picture of the competition and therefore plays down the role of innovation
- It overemphasises the importance of the wider environment and therefore ignores the significance of possible individual company advantages

IS/IT as a source of competitive advantage Pilot paper

Porter proposes three generic strategies for achieving competitive advantage.

Cost leadership means being the lowest cost producer in the industry as a whole.

Differentiation is the exploitation of a product or service which the industry as a whole believes to be unique.

Focus involves a restriction of activities to only part of the market (a segment) through.

Examples of how IS/IT can support each of these strategies are shown in the following table.

Strategy	How IS/IT can support the strategy
Cost-leadership	By facilitating reductions in cost levels, for example by reducing the number of administration staff required. Allowing better resource utilisation, for example by providing accurate stock information allowing lower 'buffer' inventories to be held. Using IT to support just-in-time and advanced manufacturing systems.
Differentiation	Differentiation can be suggested by IT, perhaps in the product itself or in the way it is marketed. The publishing example quoted earlier provides evidence of this – with the move from paper-based products to electronic.
Focus	IT may enable a more customised or specialised product/service to be produced. IT also facilitates the collection of sales and customer information that identifies targetable market segments.

Ward and Griffiths suggested four ways that IS/IT could be used for competitive advantage:

- Linking the organisation to customers or suppliers, eg EDI, website, VAN, extranet

- Creating effective integration of the use of information in a value-adding process, eg data-mining, Enterprise Resource Management
- Enabling the organisation to develop, produce, market and distribute new products or services, eg CAD, Customer Relationship Management software
- Giving senior management information to help develop and implement strategy, eg knowledge management

Peppard summarises the ways in which IT can be used for competitive advantages:

- Establishing entry barriers
- Affecting the cost of switching operations
- Differentiating products/services
- Limiting access to distribution channels
- Ensuring competitive pricing
- Decreasing supply costs
- Increasing cost efficiency
- Using information as a product
- Building closer relationships with supplies and customers

To be classed as a competitive advantage, IT linked increased productivity should not be available to others. This is unlikely unless the technology is too expensive (entry barrier), or competitors are unaware of how to utilise it.

Increased productivity may lead to reduced fixed costs. For example, fewer sales and marketing staff may be required, allowing a move to smaller premises. The effect of reduced fixed costs is shown in the following diagram.

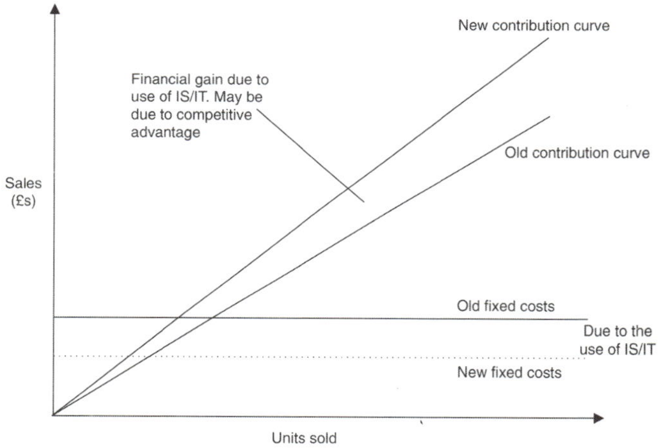

Information systems and the value chain

Michael Porter analyses the various activities of an organisation into a value chain. The value chain can be used to design a competitive strategy, by deploying the various activities strategically.

Two examples are shown below, based on two different supermarket chains.

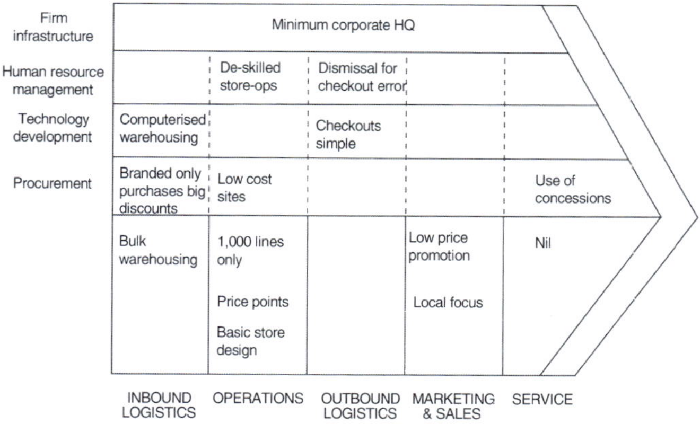
Firm infrastructure
Minimum corporate HQ
Human resource management
De-skilled store-ops
Dismissal for checkout error
Technology development
Computerised warehousing
Checkouts simple
Procurement
Branded only purchases big discounts
Low cost sites
Use of concessions
Bulk warehousing
1,000 lines only
Price points
Basic store design
Low price promotion
Local focus
Nil
INBOUND LOGISTICS
OPERATIONS
OUTBOUND LOGISTICS
MARKETING & SALES
SERVICE

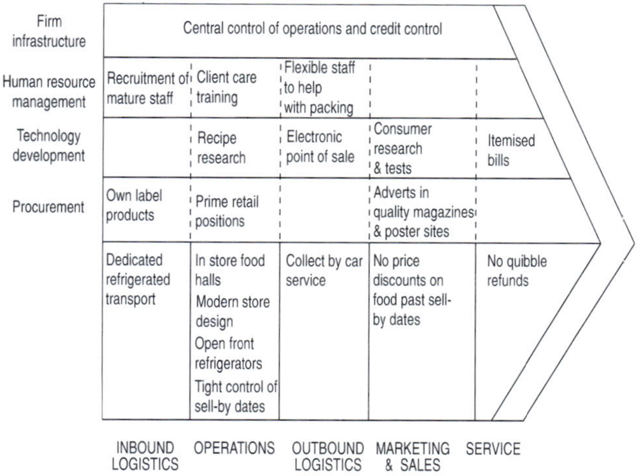
Firm infrastructure
Central control of operations and credit control
Human resource management
Recruitment of mature staff
Client care training
Flexible staff to help with packing
Technology development
Recipe research
Electronic point of sale
Consumer research & tests
Itemised bills
Procurement
Own label products
Prime retail positions
Adverts in quality magazines & poster sites
Dedicated refrigerated transport
In store food halls
Modern store design
Open front refrigerators
Tight control of sell-by dates
Collect by car service
No price discounts on food past sell-by dates
No quibble refunds
INBOUND LOGISTICS
OPERATIONS
OUTBOUND LOGISTICS
MARKETING & SALES
SERVICE

The first value chain is based on a 'discount' chain which sells on price, pursuing a cost-focus strategy. The second value chain is based on a chain which seeks to differentiate on quality and service

IT and the value chain

Value chain analysis can be used to assess the impact of IT, and to identify processes where IT could be used to add value.

- Process control. Computer systems enable tighter control over production processes
- Machine tool control. Machine tools can be automated and, it is hoped, be made more precise
- Robots can automate some of the process
- Computer aided manufacturing involves a variety of software modules
    - Production control, supervisory systems
    - Materials requirement planning (MRP) and MRP II
    - Capacity requirements planning
    - Computer integrated manufacturing (CAM) integrates all aspects of an organisation's manufacturing activities
- Flexible manufacturing systems include
    - Machine tools
    - Materials handling conveyor sets
    - Automatic guided vehicles
- Enterprise Resource Planning (ERP) systems take MRP II systems a step further, and are not restricted to certain types of organisation – they are used for identifying and

planning the enterprise-wide resources needed to record, produce, distribute, and account for customer orders

- Customer relationship management (CRM) describes the methodologies, software, and usually Internet capabilities that help an enterprise manage customer relationships

CRM consists of:

  - Helping an enterprise to identify and target their best customers, manage marketing campaigns with clear goals and objectives, and generate quality leads
  - Assisting the organisation to improve telesales, account, and sales management by optimising information shared, and streamlining existing processes
  - Allowing the formation of relationships with customers, with the aim of improving customer satisfaction and maximising profits; identifying the most profitable customers and providing them with the highest level of service
  - Providing employees with the information and processes necessary to know their customers, understand their needs, and effectively build relationships between the company, its customer base, and distribution partners

Data warehouseing

A data warehouse is a collection of data designed to support management decision making.

Data warehouses contain a wide variety of data that present a coherent picture of business conditions at a single point in time.

A 'data warehouse' is in essence a database on a very large scale: a database that can collate data stored on other, separate databases.

Data warehouse systems consist of:

- A set of programs that extract data from the operational environment
- A database that maintains data warehouse data
- Systems that provide data to users

Features of data warehouses

A data warehouse is subject-oriented, integrated, time-variant, and non-volatile.

- Subject oriented - oriented around the major 'subjects' of the enterprise such as customer, supplier, product and activity
- Integrated - data must arrive in the data warehouse in a consistent integrated state
- Time-variant - all data in the data warehouse is accurate as at some moment in time, but maybe not accurate 'now'

Data warehouse data represents data over a long time horizon – perhaps from five to ten years – whereas the operational environment typically covers current values of today up to sixty to ninety days.

Data mining

Data mining software looks for hidden patterns in a group of data. For example, data mining software can help retail companies find customers with common interests.

True data mining software does not just change the presentation, but actually discovers previously unknown relationships among the data.

> *Exam focus.* The essence of Paper 14 is how information can be used strategically.
>
> Information systems and information technology are a means towards this end.
>
> Exam questions are therefore likely to focus on how systems and technology are used, rather than simply testing your understanding of IT.

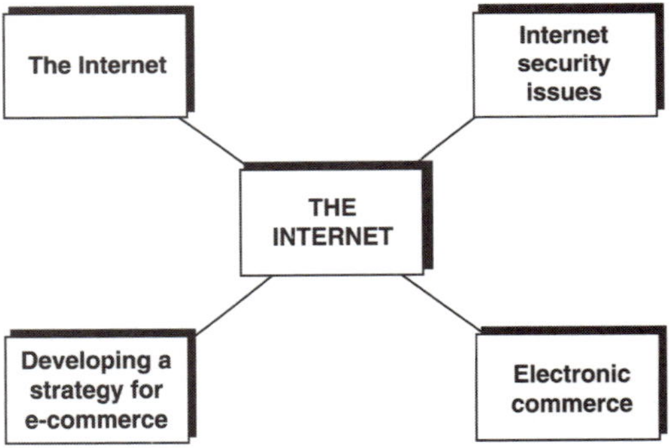

The Internet

Pilot paper

The Internet is a global network connecting millions of computers.

A **website** is a location on the Internet that provides information in text and graphic form, any of which can be viewed simply by clicking the appropriate button, word or image on the screen.

Current uses of the Internet

- Dissemination of information
- Product/service development - through almost instantaneous test marketing
- Transaction processing - both business-to-business and business-to-consumer
- Relationship enhancement - between various groups of stakeholders

- Recruitment and job search - involving organisations world-wide
- Entertainment - including music, humour, games and some less wholesome pursuits!

The impact on business

The impact of the Internet on a business sector is influenced by:

- The degree to which the customer can be persuaded to believe that using the Internet will deliver some added-value - in terms of quickness, simplicity and price
- Whether there are 'costs' which the customer has to bear - not exclusively 'costs' in the financial sense, but also such psychological 'costs' as the isolated on-line shopping experience
- The market segment to which the individual belongs - the Internet is largely the preserve of younger, more affluent, more technologically competent individuals
- The frequency of supplier/customer contact required
- The availability of incentives which might stimulate Internet acceptance

Many firms are using the Internet to exploit the transparency of supplier prices, and to **maximise their purchasing benefits** from the availability of world-wide sourcing.

Companies are also **increasing their customer service** through the web. Dell, the computer company, has created extranets for its major business customers, enabling them to receive personalised customer support, their own price lists, and some free value-added services.

Tasks which a website may automate

- Frequently-Asked Questions (FAQs)
- Status checking, major service enquiries
- Keyword search
- E-mail and systems to route and track inbound e-mail
- Customer interaction via Bulletin boards
- Call-back buttons - these enable customers to speak to someone in order to deal with and resolve a problem

WEBSITE ESSENTIALS

- Integration with all company systems (ie back office)
- Speedy implementation
- Quick and easy updating by own staff to retain topicality
- Self producing audit records
- Promotion via the internet
- Press and PR for website
- Attractive design but appropriate for the web
- Scope to interact with visitors
- Planned structure to include profitable business concept
- Control and maintenance by owner, without developer involvement

Problems with the Internet

- To a large extent the Internet has grown without any formal organisation

- The quality of much of the information on the Internet is poor
- Access and download speed is a major issue, although faster services such as Integrated Services Digital Network (ISDN) and ADSL (Asymmetric Digital Subscriber Line) are now available
- Security is perhaps the biggest worry of all

Internet security issues

Establishing organisational links to the Internet brings numerous security risks.

- Corruptions such as viruses
- Disaffected employees have much greater potential to do deliberate damage
- Hackers may be able to get into the company's internal network, either to steal data or to damage the system
- Employees may download inaccurate information or imperfect software
- Information transmitted from one part of an organisation to another may be intercepted
- The communications link itself may break down or distort data

Hacking

A hacker is a person who attempts to invade the privacy of a system. Hackers require only limited programming knowledge to cause large amounts of damage.

Hackers, in the past, have mainly been concerned to copy information, but a recent trend has been their desire to corrupt it.

Phone numbers and passwords can be guessed by hackers using password-matching software to check millions of permutations against stored passwords.

Viruses

A virus is a piece of software which infects programs and data and possibly damages them, and which replicates itself.

Viruses need an opportunity to spread. The programmers of viruses therefore place viruses in the kind of software which is most likely to be copied. This includes:

- Free software (for example from the Internet)
- Pirated software (cheaper than original versions)
- Games software (wide appeal)
- E-mail attachments (often with instructions to send the message on to others)

Viruses can spread via floppy disk, but the most destructive viruses now utilise e-mail links – travelling as attachments to e-mail messages.

Recent viruses have been programmed to send themselves to all addresses in the users electronic address book.

Jokes and hoaxes

Some mail messages or small programs claim to be doing something destructive to your computer, but are actually 'harmless' jokes.

Hoaxes usually take the form of a virus warning sent using e-mail. People pass along the warning because they are trying to be helpful, but they are wasting the time of all concerned.

Security measures

Firewalls are used to prevent unauthorised Internet users from accessing private networks connected to the Internet, especially intranets.

All messages entering or leaving the intranet pass through the firewall, which examines each message and blocks those that do not meet the specified security criteria.

Anti-virus software should be installed on all computers. All files and e-mail messages entering the system should be virus checked.

Encryption involves scrambling the data at one end of the line, transmitting the scrambled data, and unscrambling it at the receiver's end of the line.

Authentication involves adding an extra field to a record, to ensure a message has come from an authorised sender. The content of the field is derived from applying an agreed algorithm.

Dial-back security requires the user wanting access to dial in. The system then dials the person back on their authorised number before allowing them access.

The security issues surrounding e-commerce, particularly regarding making payment over the Internet are covered later.

Electronic commerce

Pilot paper

CIMA's Official Terminology defines e-commerce as 'trading on the Internet'.

Distribution

The Internet can be used to get certain products directly into people's homes. Anything that can be converted into digital form (eg text, graphics/video/sound-based products, software) can be downloaded onto the customer's PC.

Marketing

Businesses are using websites to provide information about their own products and services.

- Collecting information about customers through the use of registration schemes and cookies
- Using clickstreams by recording what users click on

What is different about the Internet and e-commerce?

- It challenges traditional business models
- It enables more product/service suppliers to interact directly with their customers
- Small companies can move instantly into a global market
- It offers a new economics of information
- It supplies virtually instant access to organisations, plus the capacity to complete purchasing transactions within seconds
- It has created new networks of communication - between organisations and their customers
- It stimulates the appearance of new intermediaries and the disappearance of some existing ones

- It promotes transparent pricing - because potential customers can readily compare prices
- It facilitates personalised attention - even if such attention is actually administered through impersonal, yet highly sophisticated IT systems
- It provides sophisticated market segmentation opportunities
- The web can either be a separate or a complementary channel

These new trends are creating pressure for companies. The main threat facing companies is that prices will be driven down by consumers' ability to shop around.

King and Clift assert that most businesses will migrate to e-business in four stages.

Stage 1. **Website**: Organisations make their presence in e-business. Attempts will be made to integrate their site's buying and selling processes into the organisation's back office systems.

Stage 2. **Connect website to supply chain**: Involves connecting the web site's capabilities to supply chains.

Stage 3. **Form alliances** to facilitate the new business model.

Stage 4. **Industrial convergence**: E-business makes it possible for industries to combine expertise and produce package solutions.

Strategic implications of e-commerce

	E-commerce	Strategic implications
Communication	The falling costs and increases in capacity of communications	Death of distance. Virtual firms can become a reality.
Business model	The traditional business model is inappropriate for e-business.	Virtual organisations will be used to capture cost savings and overthrow established practices.
IT	Existing IT systems have not adequately dealt with the customer.	Traditional IT systems will have to complement the Internet.
E-revolution	Commoditisation will make it extremely difficult for firms to differentiate their products.	Need to refine and implement new e-business strategies.
Value	The finance function does currently provide much added value in the current e-business environment.	Redesign traditional financial planning, control and evaluation techniques.

Disadvantages of e-commerce

- E-commerce involves an unusual mix of people (security people, web technology people, designers, marketing people) and can be difficult to manage

- At present, in spite of phenomenal growth the market is still fuzzy and undefined
- Many e-businesses have yet to make a profit
- Any technology installed will need to link up with existing business systems, which could be a massive undertaking
- The international availability of a website means that the laws of all countries that transactions may be conducted from have to be considered
- Trust - the lack of a physical presence is unusual and can be disconcerting

Internet merchants need to address issues such as fear of invasion of privacy and abuse of customer information (about their credit cards, for example) because they stop people even considering the Internet as a shopping medium.

Cryptography, keys and signatures

The parties involved in e-commerce need to have confidence that any communication sent gets to its target destination unchanged, and without being read by anyone else. One way of doing this is by using **electronic signatures**.

Electronic signatures can use public key (or asymmetric) cryptography. **Public key cryptography** uses two keys – public and private.

The private key is only known to its owner, and is used to scramble the data contained in a file. The 'scrambled' data is the electronic signature, and can be checked against the original file using the public key of the person who signed it.

An alternative is the use of **encryption products** that support key recovery, also known as **key encapsulation**.

Such commercial encryption products can incorporate the public key of an agent known as a **Key Recovery Agent (KRA)**. This allows the user to recover their (stored or communicated) data by approaching the KRA with an encrypted portion of the message.

Customer service on the web

Effective, competent and acceptable customer service through the web is a combination of the following factors:

- Response time
- Response quality
- Navigability
- Download times
- Security/Trust
- Order fulfilment
- Up-to-date
- Site reliability and availability
- Site effectiveness and functionality

Developing a strategy for e-commerce

In an article for IT Consultancy magazine (January-February 1999), Laurence Holt offered 18 potential strategies for e-commerce.

Strategy	Comment
Outsource to your customers	What do we do for our customers that they would rather do for themselves and could probably do better? Examples: *www.cisco.com*, *www.dell.com*.
Cannibalise your own business	If there were an Amazon.com in our market, what would it be doing? Examples: *www.barnesandnoble.com*, *www.wsj.com*.
Host your competitors	How can we create a marketplace that includes our competitors, but that we own? Examples: *www.sabre.com*, *www.jewellery.com*.
Build one-to-one customer relationships	How can we make each customer feel that we built our organisation just for them? Examples: *www.My.yahoo.com*, *www.firefly.com*, *www.netgrocer.com*.
Make first contact	What is the first step our customers take in the chain of events that leads them to buy from us? How can we make contact with them? Examples: *www.autobytel.com*.
Be a process integrator	What other things do customers need or do when they buy from us? Examples: *www.autobytel.com*.
Catch rites of passage	What major life changes are customers going through when they come into contact with us? How can we help? Examples: *www.usnews.com*, *www.citibank.com*.
Create a community	What interests do our customers share? How can we create a place that people with those interests will keep coming back to? Examples: *www.marshall.com*.
Create a niche portal	How can we make our site the portal our customers go to first? Examples: *www.tesco.net*.
Pirate your value chain	How can we take over the roles of others in our value chain? Examples: *www.dell.com*.

Strategy	Comment
Re-intermediate on information value	How can we boost the value we add through information? Examples: *www.marshall.com*.
Go pure cyberspace	What if we made the digital world our first priority and the physical world second? Examples: *www.egghead.com*.
Be a fast follower	What are our competitors doing that looks likely to be successful? How can we do the same thing faster? Examples: *www.barnesandnoble.com*.
Think dream not transaction	What dream do our customers start with that leads them to buy from us? How can we realise that dream? Examples: *www.expedia.com*.
Beat the physical world	What can we do in the digital world that would be impossible or not feasible in the physical world? Examples: *www.benjerry.com*.
Leverage the froth	What simple ideas would capture most media and public attention, even if short-lived? Examples: *www.travelocity.com*, *www.lastminute.com*.
Change the pricing model	Would our customers benefit from a different way of pricing, perhaps micro-payments or auctions? Examples: *www.priceline.com*.
Convert atoms to bits	What physical world core competencies do we have that could be applied to the digital world? Examples: *www.ups.com*.

Ten key steps to constructing an effective strategy for e-commerce

Step 1. Upgrade customer interaction

Step 2. Understand customer segments

Step 3. Understand service processes

Step 4. Define the role of the site

Step 5. Decide on the technology

Step 6. Ensure you can deal with the new volume of customer interaction

Step 7. Create incentives

Step 8. Decide on channel choices

Step 9. Exploit the Internet to create new relationships

Step 10. Implement

Exam focus. It is extremely likely that at least one question in the exam will require some understanding of how businesses can utilise the Internet and websites.

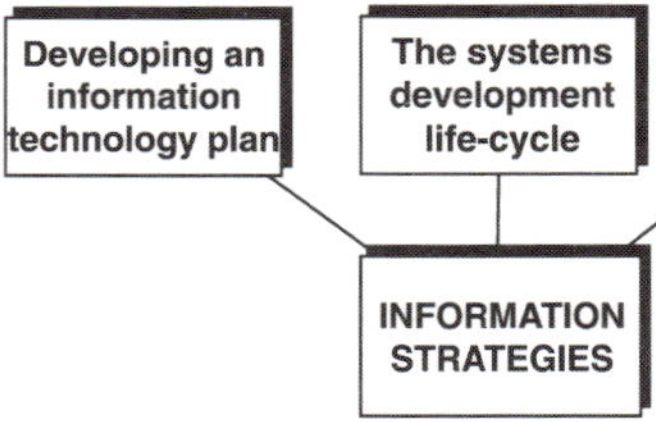

Developing an information technology plan

An organisation's information technology strategy and plan should reflect its business strategy, and match its information technology needs.

The International Federation of Accountants, through its Information Technology Committee identifies **ten principles an information technology management plan should be based on**.

1. Alignment

The IT strategy must be consistent with the needs and direction of the organisation. To achieve this alignment, the key drivers of the information technology strategy should be the targets identified in the overall organisation strategic plan.

2. Scope

The scope of the information technology plan has a major impact on the effort required to prepare it, as well as the plan's acceptance and ultimate success.

Issues to consider include links with other business or functional strategies.

3. Time frame

Information technology initiatives can take a long period to implement. The timeframe will vary according to the type of the industry and an organisations circumstances.

4. Cost-benefit justification

Costs of implementation must be less than the combined tangible and intangible benefits expected to be realised. The implementation of information technologies can lead to considerable cost savings or other strategic benefits, for example, increased market share through better service delivery. These benefits, both tangible and intangible, must be realised if an organisation is to receive value-for-money from its information technology investments.

5. Achievability

Information technology related initiatives could require major investments in terms of capital and people. It is essential that the plan is realistic given the resources available.

6. Monitoring and control

The plan should provide a basis for measuring and monitoring performance. A successful plan must provide a yardstick for measuring progress and serve as a benchmark for modifying objectives to improve and provide input for corrective action - either to improve performance or revise the plan. Typically, an information technology plan will provide performance milestones against which performance can be measured.

7. Reassessment

Plans are based on business and information technology assumptions. If these assumptions change, the existing initiatives and projects may be inappropriate, or more effective alternatives may have emerged. An effective plan must be flexible and provide for periodic reassessment of the validity and effectiveness of both strategies and tactics.

8. Awareness

Once the information technology plan has been approved, it should be disseminated to all concerned.

9. Accountability

All plans require translation into action. Responsibility for the implementation, execution and monitoring of the plan should be explicit.

10. Commitment

The implementation of the projects contained in the plan may require significant resources. These resources are only likely to be available on a timely basis if there is strong support for the plan and its objectives from senior management.

The systems development life-cycle

In the early days of computing, systems development was piecemeal, involving automation of existing procedures rather than forming part of a planned strategy.

The consequences were often poorly designed systems, which cost too much and which were not suited to users' needs.

In the 1960s the National Computing Centre developed a more disciplined approach to systems development - this approach became known as the Systems Development Life Cycle (SDLC).

There are six stages, although in practice stages may overlap.

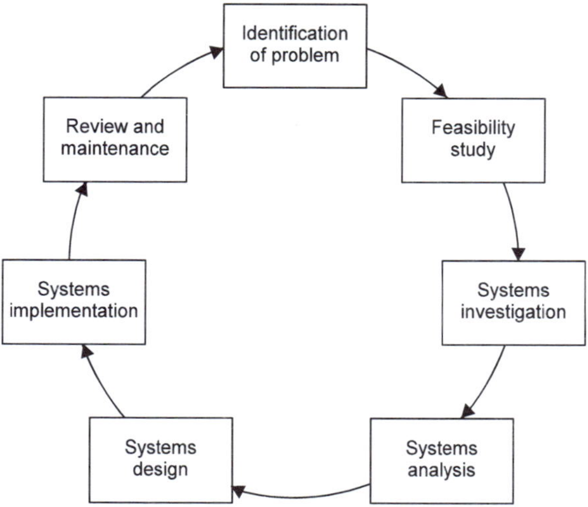

SYSTEMS DEVELOPMENT LIFE CYCLE	
Feasibility study	Briefly review the existing system Identify possible alternative solutions
Systems investigation	Obtain details of current requirements and user needs such as data volumes, processing cycles and timescales Identify current problems and restrictions
Systems analysis	Consider why current methods are used and identify better alternatives
Systems design	Determine what inputs, processing and storage facilities are necessary to produce the outputs required Consider matters such as program design, file design and security Prepare a detailed specification of the new system.
Systems implementation	Write or acquire software, test it, convert files, install hardware and start running the new system
Review and maintenance	Ensure that the new system meets current objectives, and that it continues to do so

The cycle begins again when a review suggests that it is becoming difficult for an installed system to continue to meet current objectives through routine maintenance.

Drawbacks of the SDLC

The SDLC approach has some drawbacks, particularly if it is not properly implemented.

- Neglects management information through an over-emphasis on automating clerical tasks
- Discourages innovation through automating existing methodologies rather than seeking new ones
- User opinions are often under-valued resulting in dissatisfied users
- Incomplete systems often resulted where unique processing situations could not be automated
- Time overruns are almost expected!

Systems development methodologies

One approach that should avoid the drawbacks of the SDLC is to use *a systems development methodology.*

A systems development methodology is a collection of procedures, techniques, tools and documentation aids used when implementing a new information system.

Different methodologies emphasise different aspects of the development process. Soft systems methodology (SSM) concentrates on establishing what problems the system should solve. Structured methodologies such as Structured Systems Analysis and Design (SSADM) emphasises the design of solutions.

There are three underlying approaches.

- **Process-driven** methodologies emphasise activities or functions of the system. Example: Structured Systems Analysis and Design Methodology (SSADM)
- **Data-driven** methodologies emphasise data in a system, which is less likely to change than the processes which act on it. Example: information engineering
- **User-driven** methodologies focus on behavioural aspects of systems design. They recognise the importance of user involvement and encourage active participation. Example: Soft Systems Methodology (SSM)

Advantages of methodologies are as follows.

- There is a strict framework of reporting stages
- Outputs from each stage are specified
- Tools and techniques are available
- Documentation standards are rigorous

Disadvantages also exist.

- Some are limited in scope, conceptual basis and regard for the work/social context
- They are tailored towards very large systems
- They are better for transaction processing systems than management information systems
- Modern techniques such as prototyping and fourth generation languages may not fit with a methodology

Exam focus. Methodologies are one way of attempting to involve users in the development process.

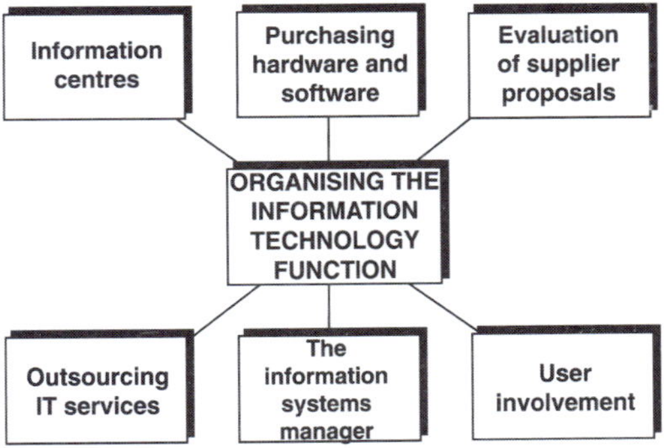

Information centres

Information centre

An information centre (IC) is a unit of staff with a good technical awareness of computer systems, who provide a support function to computer users within the organisation. The IC may have responsibility for approving all information system related purchases.

Help-desk

An IC usually offers some kind of help-desk.

Problem solving

The IC will maintain a record of problems and identify those that occur most often.

Improvements

The IC can also consider the viability of suggestions for improvements.

Standards and procedures

The IC is also likely to be responsible for setting, and encouraging users to conform to, common standards, for example:

- Hardware standards
- Software standards
- Programming standards
- Processing standards
- Security and back-up procedures

Purchasing hardware and software

An organisation may issue an **invitation to tender** to a range of suppliers, setting out the following.

- The volume of data to be processed
- The complexity of processing requirements
- The number and geographical spread of users
- Response times required
- Expected inputs and outputs
- Future plans of the organisation

The invitation should also provide details of the following.

- Contact within the organisation
- Financial constraints
- Closing date for submission
- Expected form of submission (including address)

Financing methods

- Purchase
  - Important matters related to software support, maintenance and warranties
- Leasing
  - Finance lease – the user is in effect repaying the full value of the equipment to the lessor. The assets are the possessions of lessees, although the lessor retains title to them.
  - Under operating leases the lessor does not expect to recover the capital cost of the equipment over the lease term. They tend to offer extra benefits over finance leases, and might be more flexible. Many offer upgrading facilities.
- Rental
  - Usually involves a fixed charge payable over a set period
  - Is relatively expensive
  - Payments are simply charged against profit as incurred
  - Allow certainty in financial planning
  - Obsolescence is not a concern

Features of leasing

- Payment spread over time
- Maintenance costs and the costs of rectifying faulty equipment are generally included under operating leases
- The interest payment is fixed in advance
- The lessor owns the asset, and can repossess it if payments are not made

- A lessor's criteria for lending may be less strict than other lenders
- An operating lease may permit the lessee to terminate the contract

Evaluation of supplier proposals

Possible approaches include

- Identifying an existing customer with similar profile/ workload
- Benchmark tests
- Simulation tests

Suppliers' proposals need to be evaluated. Comparison may be difficult.

- The supplier should be encouraged to identify an existing customer with a similar profile/workload, if possible
- Key factors might be identified and weighted in order of importance

Benchmark tests

These test how long it takes a machine to run through a particular set of programs. More powerful machines will do the processing more quickly.

Simulation tests

Simulation testing uses *synthetic programs* written specifically for testing purposes and incorporating routines designed to test a variety of situations.

Other factors

Other factors include reliability, warranty and maintenance, support, training and upgrading.

Key considerations in the choice of both hardware and software are

- User requirements
- Cost
- Compatibility

Hardware

The choice of computer hardware will usually depend on:

- User requirements
- Power
- Reliability
- Simplicity
- Flexibility
- Security
- Cost
- Changeover
- Software requirements
- Maintenance agreement

Software selection

The main option facing an organisation is whether to buy off-the-shelf software or have it specially written (bespoke), either in-house or by a third party.

- Bespoke
  - Written or adapted by software house or in-house
  - More expensive
  - Likely to match requirements more closely
  - Required for complex/unusual applications
  - Will require greater testing – more likely to have 'bugs'
  - May be a long delay before the software is ready
- Off-the-shelf
  - Standard solution which may be suitable
  - Written by specialists
  - Good documentation and support
  - Track record
  - Available for mainstream applications
  - Available now
  - Cheaper
  - May not meet requirements exactly – although some customisation may be possible

The choice of software depends on the following additional factors.

- Processing times
- Documentation
- User-friendliness
- Controls
- Up-to-dateness
- Modifiability
- Other users
- Support and maintenance

User involvement *Pilot paper*

There are a number of approaches that help to ensure adequate of user involvement in the development process.

Structured walkthroughs

Structured walkthroughs are used by analysts to present their design to interested user groups – in other words to 'walk' them through the design.

Structured walkthroughs are formal meetings, in which the documentation produced during development is reviewed and checked for errors or omissions.

The importance of signing off work

At the end of each stage of development, the resulting output is presented to users for their approval. There must be a formal sign-off of each completed stage before work on the next stage begins.

Joint applications development

Joint Applications Development (JAD) is based on a partnership between users and IT specialists.

JAD was originally developed by IBM to promote a more participative approach to systems. The potential value to an organisation may be as follows.

- Creates a pool of expertise comprised of interested parties from all relevant functions
- Reduced risk of systems 'imposed' by computer systems personnel
- Increases user ownership and responsibility for systems

- Emphasises the information needs of users and their relationship to business needs and decision making

Possible risks affecting the potential value of JAD:

- The relative inexperience of many users may lead to misunderstandings and possibly unreasonable expectations
- The danger of lack of co-ordination leading to fragmented systems

Rapid applications development

JAD may also be used as a tool for users and IT specialists to build software using Rapid Applications Development (RAD).

RAD can be described as a quick way of building software. It combines a management approach to systems development with the use of modern software tools such as graphics-based user interfaces and object oriented design methods.

Prototyping

A prototype is a model of all or part of a system, built to show users early in the design process how it will appear.

Using prototyping software, the programmer can write an application program quickly.

He or she can then check with the data user whether the prototype program that has been designed appears to meet the user's needs, and if it doesn't it can be amended.

The advantages of prototyping are as follows.

- Enables a 'mock-up' version to be seen by users early in the development process

- It makes efficient use of programmer time by helping programmers to develop programs more quickly

Disadvantages of prototyping.

- Many prototyping software tools cannot 'travel' from one system to another
- It is sometimes argued that prototyping encourages inefficient use of program code
- Computer users may be unimaginative, requesting a system similar to what they already have
- Some say prototyping tools allow programmers to produce shoddy programs quickly

User groups

A user group is a forum for users of particular hardware or, more usually, software, so that they can share ideas and experience.

The term is commonly associated with users of existing packaged software who wish to contribute ideas for the continuing development and improvement of packages.

Sometimes user groups are set up within individual organisations.

Management support

A successful system implementation requires management commitment and support.

Steering committees

Some organisations have a steering committee to oversee the use of IT. Common responsibilities include:

- To approve (or reject) IT projects
- To establish company guidelines within the framework of the IT strategy for the development of computer based processing and management information systems
- The evaluation of the feasibility study reports and system specifications
- To monitor and review each new system after implementation
- Assessing the contribution of each project to the long term corporate objectives of the organisation

The steering committee might include the following.

- The information director, or a senior IS staff member
- Accountants for advice relating to costs and benefits
- Management from affected departments

The information systems manager

The manager in charge of information systems needs the following skills.

- General management ability
- An understanding of organisational activities and functions
- Technical expertise in developing and running information systems

Strategy

The information systems manager is responsible for ensuring that the organisation's acquisition and use of information technology and computer systems fits in with the goals and objectives of the organisation as a whole.

Information infrastructure

The information systems manager should ensure that IT systems activities undertaken by users should firstly satisfy user demands and secondly be aligned with the overall system goals and organisational objectives.

This activity will include overall responsibility for the construction of an information infrastructure comprising:

- Technical standards
- Software standards
- Establishment of corporate databases
- Providing an information systems service function

Liaison

Liaison between information systems professionals and the rest of the organisation is a key role.

The environment

Interaction with the environment is important. This is essential for a strategic perspective.

Constraints on strategy development

There are a variety of constraints an information systems manager may have to contend with.

- Shortage of skilled staff
- Backlogs in application development due to previous time over-runs
- The pressure for continued expansion

The information systems manager needs to be able to travel between **two worlds**: the organisation as a whole, its culture, internal politics and strategic objectives, and the specialised world of information technology.

Outsourcing IT services

There is a range of available external resources and services.

Facilities management

Computer operations can be contracted out (outsourced) to a FM organisation. This may range from contracting out development to handing over the full running of entire computing operations.

- Advantages
  - Economies of scale
  - Fixed (predictable) price
  - Access to expertise
- Disadvantages
  - Arguably, loss of control over a part of the business which may be critical to future strategy
  - It is difficult to reverse the decision
  - The level of *service* is fixed

Other organisations

- Software houses offer
  - Systems analysis and design
  - Bespoke software services
  - Applications packages and support
- Consultants offer a range of general and specialised services
- Computer manufacturers help with
  - Provision and installation of equipment
  - Maintenance

Advantages of facilities management

- It is an effective form of cost control, as there is often a long-term contract where services are specified in advance for a fixed price
- Long-term contracts (maybe up to ten years) allow for greater certainty in planning
- A facilities management company has economies of scale
- Skills and knowledge are not lost through in-house IT staff leaving
- New skills and knowledge become available
- Resources employed can be scaled up or down depending upon demand

Disadvantages

- It is arguable that information and its provision is an inherent part of the business and too important to be contracted out

- To let outsiders handle information processing could be seen as highly risky in commercial and/or legal terms
- Opportunities to use IS for competitive advantage may be missed if a third party is handling IS services
- The contract may not be flexible enough
- The use of FM does not encourage a proper awareness of the potential costs and benefits of IT

The contract

A vital aspect of any FM contract is the service level contract (SLC). This should specify:

- Minimum levels of service
- Exactly what services will be provided
- Security and confidentiality responsibilities
- Arrangements for an exit route

Exam focus. An optional question in the Pilot Paper required recommendations regarding how the information systems infrastructure could facilitate meeting user requirements.

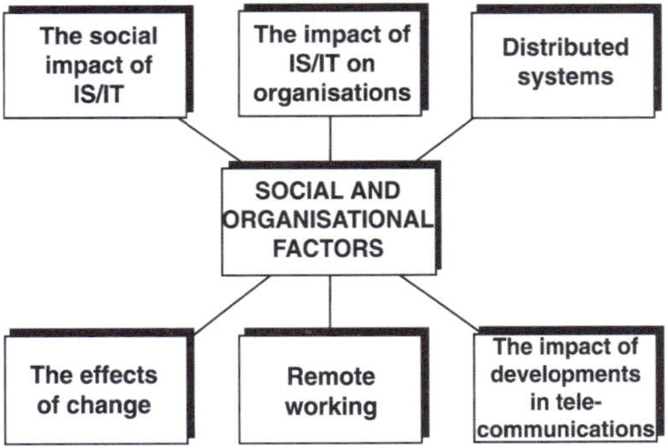

The social impact of IS/IT

The pace of change in modern society, and in the business environment in particular, continues to accelerate.

The first wave

The world changed from a hunting and gathering culture to an agricultural age.

The hunting and gathering stage lasted a million years, the agricultural age lasted six thousand years.

The second wave

The world changed from an agricultural based planet to a world defined by the industrial revolution.

The third wave

The third wave is the present change from the industrial age to the communications age. As this shift occurs, we can expect life to speed up even more and we can anticipate new patterns of human interaction.

Wealth in the communications age is linked to **knowledge**. The rich and powerful of our era will be those who find ways to turn raw data (information) into usable knowledge.

Social changes

The move to a **communications age** requires that visions of the future be adaptable, that long-range plans be flexible, and that we build in mechanisms for adjusting to change.

The Internet offers an alternative way of doing business, and as e-commerce increases the following social phenomena are likely to be observed.

- **Travel**

  People can obtain what they want without leaving their desk. This should make shops and roads less crowded. In the long-term it may affect where people choose to live.

- **Consumer choice**

  A computer search for an item or service can be done in seconds. Consumers are also not restricted to local providers.

- **The 'size' of society**

  Society itself becomes global. People do business in places and with organisations that they would never have considered or even known about before.

- **Time management and quality of life**

  Rather than being restricted to business hours people can obtain what they want 24 hours a day.

- **Interaction**

  Instead of dealing face-to-face or voice-to-voice with others, people interact with their computer.

- **Work opportunities**

  There will be fewer opportunities for people to work in sales roles that involve direct contact with others, but greater opportunities to work in distribution and transport.

The impact if IS/IT on organisations

Pilot paper

Modern communications technology makes decentralised organisations possible.

Control is being passed down the line to workers or outsourced to external companies.

We are moving towards an 'e-lance economy', which will be characterised by shifting coalitions of freelancers and small firms collaborating on particular projects.

The organisational implications of office automation

Office automation has affected organisations in a variety of ways.

- Routine processing of data can be done in bigger volumes, at greater speed and with greater accuracy
- Files are more likely to be magnetic files or microform files rather than paper files
- Office staff must show a greater computer awareness
- Managers may have to learn to work at a workstation
- Managers have access to more information

- Planning activities should be more thorough, with the use of models
- Information for control should be more readily available
- Decision making by managers can be helped by decision support systems
- Multi-user and distributed systems put more information into local offices encouraging decentralisation
- The pace of technological change in computer hardware and software commit an organisation to continual change
- Customer service should improve as information retrieval is quicker

Power and privacy

The power of computer systems makes them a threat to the privacy of the individual.

Privacy is the right of the individual to control the user of information about him or her.

Most countries have introduced legislation designed to protect the individual. In the UK the current legislation is the Data Protection Act 1998.

From another point of view information is a source of **power** in an organisation. If you know something that your colleagues do not, you have the power to exploit that knowledge for your own ends.

Interoperability

Interoperability means that any company, individual or institution can readily share and exchange information and facilities with any other company, individual or institution.

Backward compatibility

A new version of a program is said to be backward compatible if it can use files and data created with an older version of the same program.

Backward compatibility is important because it eliminates the need to start afresh when upgrading to a newer product.

Legacy system

A legacy system is a computer system that continues to be used because of the prohibitive cost of replacing or redesigning it.

Open systems

Open systems aim to ensure compatibility between different systems to encourage interaction. An open systems infrastructure supports organisation-wide functions and allows interoperability of networks and systems.

Distributed systems

The structure of an organisation and the way in which the organisation's computer system is configured are related issues.

- **Centralised** processing involves data processing in a single location such as a computer centre at head office.
- **Decentralised** or distributed processing utilises the power of a number of connected processors. ('Decentralised' emphasises organisational/ control aspects, while 'distributed' emphasises processing aspects.)
  - Computers are distributed over various locations
  - Files may be held locally
  - Processing may be done centrally and/or locally

  - Reliance on a single processor is eliminated
  - Flexibility is increased
  - Users are more involved

Multi-user systems

These involve the connection of a number of users to the same (centralised) computer. Each user has their own terminal and apparently simultaneous access to the processor. Benefits, compared with stand-alone computers, are as follows.

- Increased access to the central computer
- High processing speeds
- Some departmental control, eg over input documents

Distributed systems

A distributed system is a combination of processing hardware located at a central place, with other, usually smaller, computers located at other sites. The central and dispersed computers are linked by a communications network.

Benefits of distributed processing:

- Organisational flexibility is increased: new components can be added easily
- Patterns of traditional computing are reversed: the desktop becomes the focus of attention
- Workgroups become the focal point, bridging the gap between department and individual
- Dispersed organisational structures are supported

Disadvantages of distributed processing include:

- Possible data duplication
- Administration may be more complex
- Possible compatibility issues

Networks

A network is an interconnected series of *autonomous* computers. A network operating system allows users to share facilities.

- Data, ie files on various hard disks on the network
- Resources, eg peripherals such as printers
- Programs

LANs

Local area networks are usually located on a single site or in a single building. Computers are linked by cables. There is often a server computer, such as a file server.

There are various topologies.

- Bus
- Ring
- Star
- Tree

WANs

Wide area networks are spread over a larger geographical area. They may incorporate LANs.

Data is transmitted over telecommunications links using modems or ISDN links.

Client-server computing

This term describes the relationship between devices in a network. Tasks are distributed between the machines on the network.

- The client is the machine that requests the service
- The server is the machine dedicated to providing a particular function or service requested by the client. Servers include file servers, print servers and fax servers
- Processing power is distributed to where it is most needed
- A network computer (NC) has no hard disk. It downloads applications and data from a powerful server or from the Internet

Downsizing

Allied to the introduction and widespread adoption of distributed processing is downsizing. This involves moving from a centralised mainframe to networks of minicomputers or PCs.

- The same processing power is achieved at a lower cost by buying cheaper technology and decentralising processing
- It is not always appropriate; many business needs involve centralised 'number-crunching'

Reasons for downsizing include the following.

- A wish to move away from mainframes, which may originally have been the only choice available

- A change of strategy for information use
- Cost cutting
  - It is questionable whether this is achievable
  - Mainframe costs are well defined
  - There are hidden costs (security, support, management) in distributed systems

The impact of developments in communications

Pilot paper

Electronic mail (E-mail)

The term 'electronic mail' or e-mail is used to describe various systems of sending data or messages electronically via a telephone or data network and a central computer.

E-mail has the following advantages.

- Speed
- Economy
- Efficiency (a message is prepared once but can be sent to thousands of employees at the touch of a button)
- Security (access can be restricted by the use of passwords)
- Electronic delivery and read receipts can be requested
- Attachments are supported eg a spreadsheet file

Each user will typically have password protected access to his own inbox, outbox and filing system.

Drawbacks of e-mail

- Non-literal messages are not conveyed

- All exchanges are recorded
- They are often received at a time when they can not be given the instant attention the sender expects
- People stop talking to each other!
- Staff may quickly find themselves suffering from information overload
- Staff may spend excessive amounts of time dealing with personal e-mail

Voice mail

Voice mail (or v-mail) systems enable the caller's message to be recorded at the recipient's voice mailbox similar to a mailbox in an e-mail system. A voice mail message is basically a spoken memo.

Voice messaging

This is a kind of switchboard answerphone that takes the place of a human receptionist, or at least relieves the receptionist of the burden of dealing with common, straightforward calls.

Computer Telephony Integration (CTI) systems gather information about callers such as their telephone number and customer account number or demographic information (age, income, interests etc).

This is stored on a customer database and can be called up and sent to the screen of the person dealing with the call, perhaps before the call has even been put through.

Computer conferencing

With a computer conferencing system there is a huge central mailbox where messages can be deposited for everyone to see.

Computer conferencing can be appropriate for a team of individuals at different locations to compare notes – similar to bulletin boards.

Videoconferencing

Videoconferencing is the use of computer and communications technology to conduct meetings in which several participants, perhaps in different parts of the world, are linked up via computer and a video system.

Even if the technology used is expensive, it is far cheaper when compared to the cost in management time and air fares of business travel.

Drawbacks of videoconferencing

Videoconferencing allows far more frequent face to face contact between people who are spread widely across the world, but it does present some difficulties.

- Cultural differences might be forgotten
- The technology currently offered by some providers of videoconferencing facilities is far from perfect. Frequently there are problems with the synchronisation of lip movement and speech and with body language such as hand movements
- The systems tend to be voice-activated, and this means that the camera gives priority to the person speaking the loudest

- Some people feel less need to participate when attending this sort of meeting

> *Exam focus.* Be aware of the suitability, advantages and disadvantages of electronic communication in different situations.

Remote working *Pilot paper*

Advances in communications technology have, for some tasks, reduced the need for the actual presence of an individual in the office.

The advantages to the organisation of homeworking include:

- Cost savings on space
- A larger pool of labour. The possibility of working at home might attract more applicants for clerical positions

The advantages to the individual of homeworking are:

- No time is wasted commuting
- Work can be organised flexibly
- Possibly less interruptions

The problems for the organisation are chiefly problems of control

Other 'problems' for the organisation might be as follows.

- Co-ordination of the work of different homeworkers
- Training
- Building organisational culture

Problems for homeworkers are as follows.

- Isolation
- Intrusions
- Adequate space
- Adequate facilities and equipment
- Homeworkers, especially if they are freelances, have fewer employment rights

The effects of change

Change may affect people in several ways.

Physiological changes - as the natural product of ageing or due to external factors eg sleeping patterns due to night work.

Circumstantial changes - establishing new relationships, working to new routines.

Change often leads to **uncertainty** and **insecurity**.

Resistance to change

Sources of resistance to change itself may include age and inflexibility, strong needs for security, emotional instability etc.

There are four common causes of resistance.

- Self-interest
- Misunderstanding
- Contradictory assessments
- Low tolerance of change itself

Reactions to proposed change may range from the following.

- Acceptance
- Indifference
- Passive resistance
- Active resistance

Achieving change in the workplace

Resistance should be welcomed and confronted, not swept under the carpet.

Talking thorough areas of conflict may lead to useful insights and the adapting of the programme of change to advantage.

- There should be free circulation of **information** about the reasons for the change, its expected results and likely consequences
- The change must be '**sold**' to the people: people must be convinced that their attitudes and behaviours need changing
- People should be **reassured** that they have the learning capacity, the ability and the resources to implement the plan
- **Learning programmes** for any new skills or systems necessary will have to be designed according to the abilities, previous learning experience etc of the individuals concerned
- The effects of insecurity, perceived helplessness, and therefore resentment, will reduced if the people can be **involved** in the planning and implementation of the change

Human factors in IS/IT systems development

IT is by nature an area that changes constantly. Particular concerns of employees that will need to be addressed include:

- Job security and status
- Retaining efficient access to information needed to perform their job
- Career prospects

User involvement in the development process is crucial to dispel these fears.

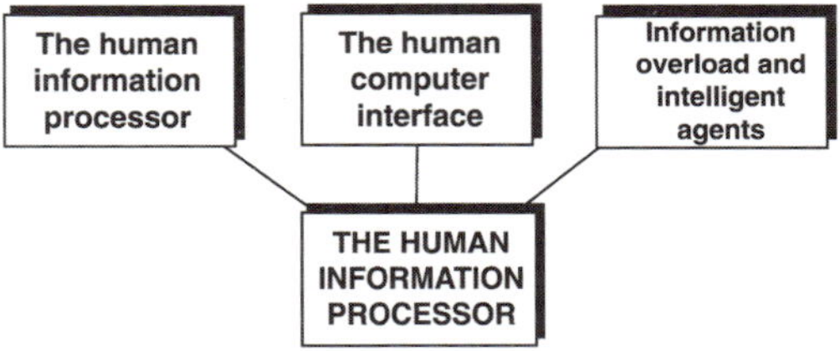

The human information processor

The term 'human information processor' describes the process by which people receive, interpret and respond to their environment.

Simple model

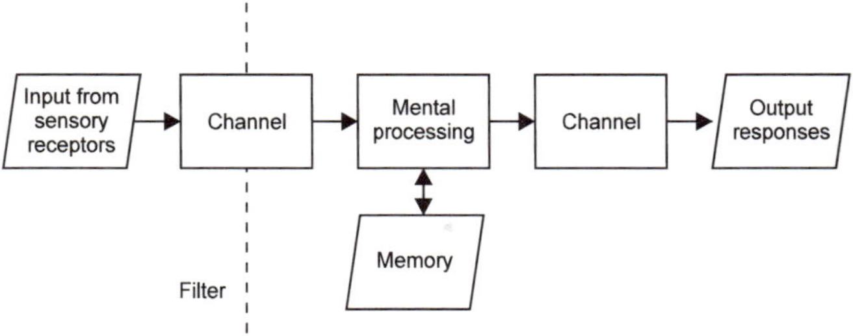

- Sensory receptors: eyes and ears pick up signals and transmit them to the processing unit
- Processor: this is the brain, which includes storage capability
- Output consists of spoken and written responses

The world provides far more input than the human processing system can deal with.

If capacity is exceeded, information overload can result in deterioration in processing

The system must therefore filter in various ways.

- By reference to the individual's personal experience and background
  - Humans establish patterns of data to support their understanding of a situation
  - The frame of reference eliminates the need to develop a new routine each time
- By standardising decision procedures
  - Decision making follows established rules
  - Inputs perceived to be irrelevant are simply ignored

Where a decision is made under stress, filtering is increased. The focus is on the most important matters and stimuli relating to less important matters are ignored.

Newell-Simon model

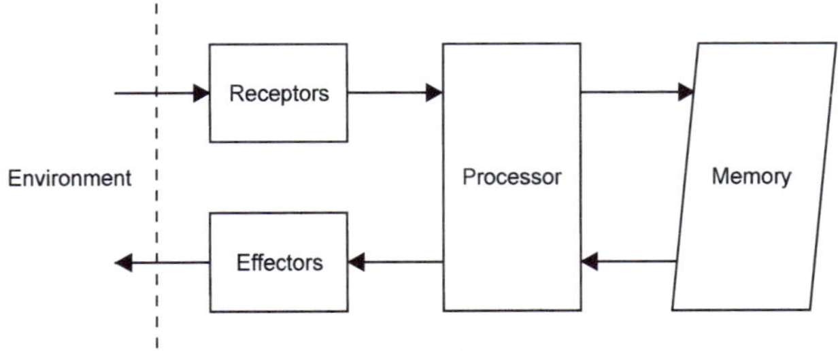

- Sensory input, processor and output are as above

- Memory has three components
  - Long-term memory's capacity essentially unlimited
  - Short-term memory is small, for example it can cope only with phone numbers or 'seven, plus or minus two'
  - External memory uses external media such as a notepad

Human information processing strategies

Strategies may be developed to overcome human processors' limitations

- Concreteness focuses on keywords and uses information which is readily available and requires no search or manipulation
- Anchoring and adjustment requires the establishment of an anchor point and then adjustment from this (for example budgeting)

  Choosing an inappropriate anchor and undervaluation of new evidence in making adjustments may cause problems

The human computer interface

The human computer interface is a set of commands or menus through which a user communicates with a program.

Input design

There is a balance between the requirements of the system and the capabilities of users.

Factors to consider include the following.

- Volume of input
- Frequency of input

- Location of data collection/capture
- Input medium and the need for transcription
- Data verification
- Data validation

Output design

Printouts and screens must be well designed if the system is to be fully utilised. Factors to consider include:

- Frequency of output
- Volume of output
- Sequence of production
- Output medium

There are three broad techniques by which a user can provide instructions/enter data.

- Menu systems involve the selection of the required item from hierarchical lists
- With form filling the screen may mirror the source document. The cursor moves to the next field as each entry is completed
- Graphical user interfaces, with Windows, Icons, Mouse-clicking and Pull-down menus (WIMP), are now the norm

User friendliness

The easier a package is to use, the more efficient it (and the user) will be. The following features all improve the user-friendliness of a system.

- Ease of data entry
- Intuitiveness
- Consistent design
- On-screen help
- Use of dialogue boxes and on-screen prompts
- Escapability
- Customisation

The working environment

The ability of people to process information is influenced by their environment.

The physical environment can influence people through:

- The health and safety of workers
- Enabling performance
- Fostering organisational culture

Ergonomics

Ergonomics is the study of the relationship between people and the working environment. The aim is to establish working conditions that are best suited to the capacities and requirements of the human body.

Ergonomics includes the design of office equipment so that, for example, chairs and desks are designed to be comfortable and supportive.

Information overload and intelligent agents *Pilot paper*

Information overload

Computing and communications developments have led to the capture and transmission of ever increasing amounts of information.

An excess of irrelevant information is harmful - a person is more likely to miss or miss-interpret vital information after being swamped with irrelevant material.

There are two main approaches to avoiding information overload.

- Firstly, the characteristics of the information passed to a human information processor need to be considered
- Secondly the number of information sources feeding an individual can be managed

The qualities of information were covered in Chapter 1.

Limiting the number of information sources

The approach taken to limiting the sources of information will depend on the situation. In some instances it may be sufficient to implement temporary measures to delay non-urgent information reaching a person, other situations may require a permanent change.

- Delegate to colleagues
- Review reports received for information duplication
- Re-route incoming telephone calls
- Use voice-mail

- Filter incoming e-mail
- Use an Internet news-clipping service
- Use intelligent agents

Intelligent agents

Intelligent agents are programs that perform tasks such as retrieving and delivering information and automating repetitive tasks.

Intelligent agent software can be applied to monitor an individual's use of a computerised system and 'learn' what the user wants and does not want to know from what he does day-by-day.

Interface agents employ artificial intelligence techniques in order to provide assistance to a user dealing with a particular application. A fairly primitive example is the Office Assistant in the Microsoft Office package.

An **information agent** is able to collate and manipulate information obtained from various sources to answer queries posed by users and other information agents. Finding a solution to a query might involve an agent accessing information sources over a network or over the Internet.

Exam focus. Information overload fits the Paper 14 syllabus very well – and is therefore a likely subject for examination.

Notes

Leigh Ingleby

Core Management

Managing in a Business Context

First edition 2004

ISBN 0 7517 1474 7

British Library Cataloguing-in-Publication Data

A catalogue record for this book is available from the British Library

Published by

BPP Professional Education, Aldine House, Aldine Place, London W12 8AW

www.bpp.com

Printed in Great Britain by Ashford Colour Press

Welcome to BPP's **Passcards.**

- They **save you time**. Important topics are summarised for you.
- They incorporate **diagrams** to kick start your memory.
- BPP's **Passcards** are not just a condensed book. Each card has been separately designed for clear presentation. Topics are self-contained and can be grasped visually.
- **Passcards** are still **just the right size** for pockets, briefcases and bags.
- **Passcards focus on the exam** you will be facing.

Passcards are a **complement** to other study materials that you have been using and together with question practice will help you prepare for success.

Run through the complete set of **Passcards** as often as you can during your final revision period. The day before the exam, try to go through the **Passcards** again! You will then be well on your way to passing your exams.

Good luck!

Preface

Contents

1: Strategy and the business context

Topic List

- What is strategy?
- The rational model
- Emergent strategies
- Muddling through
- Learning organisations

Constant changes in the external environment mean that managers have to develop and adapt strategy in order that their organisations can survive and remain competitive. Managers of private, public and voluntary sectors will seek to minimise threats to the business and maximise opportunities when disturbances occur.

It is essential to have a thorough understanding of how organisations approach the strategic planning process. Make sure you understand the nature and role of strategy, how strategy is put into practice and the part stakeholders play in influencing strategic decisions.

Johnson and Scholes describe strategy as

'the direction and scope of an organisation over the long term which achieves advantage... through its configuration of resources within a changing environment to meet the needs of markets and to fulfil stakeholder expectations'

Direction + Scope
Long Term
Achieves Advantage
Changing Environment
Market Needs
Fulfil Stakeholders expectations

Strategy

A course of action, including the specification of resources required, to meet a specific objective.

Tactics

The **deployment** of resources to execute an agreed strategy.

Policy

A general statement providing guidelines for the management of decision making.

Strategic management

The development, implementation and control of agreed strategies.

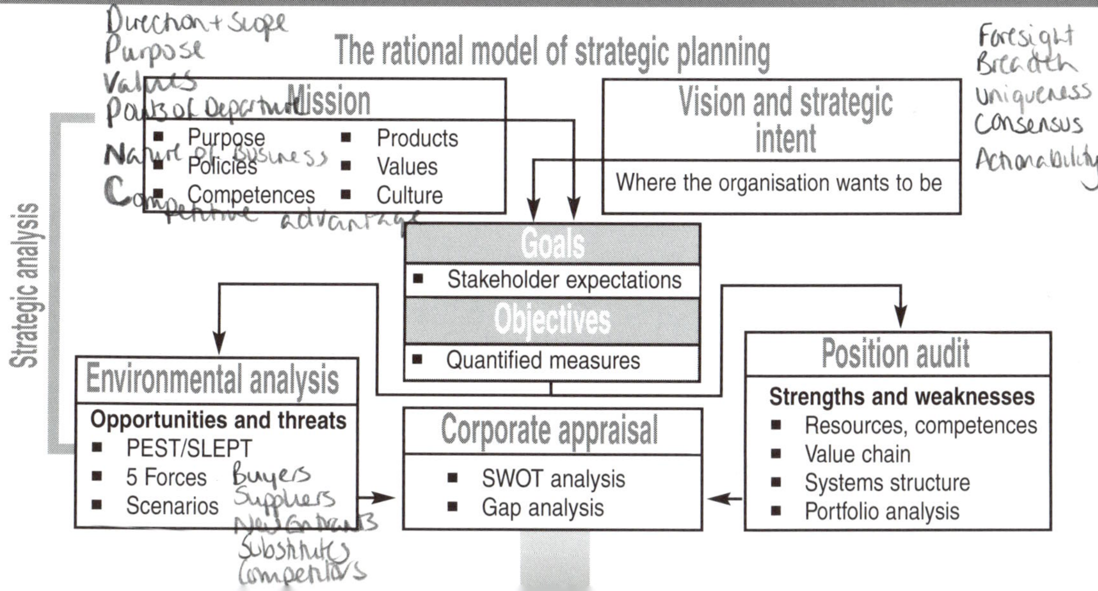
The rational model of strategic planning
Mission
Purpose
Policies
Competences
Products
Values
Culture
Vision and strategic intent
Where the organisation wants to be
Goals
Stakeholder expectations
Objectives
Quantified measures
Environmental analysis
Opportunities and threats
PEST/SLEPT
5 Forces
Scenarios
Corporate appraisal
SWOT analysis
Gap analysis
Position audit
Strengths and weaknesses
Resources, competences
Value chain
Systems structure
Portfolio analysis
Strategic analysis

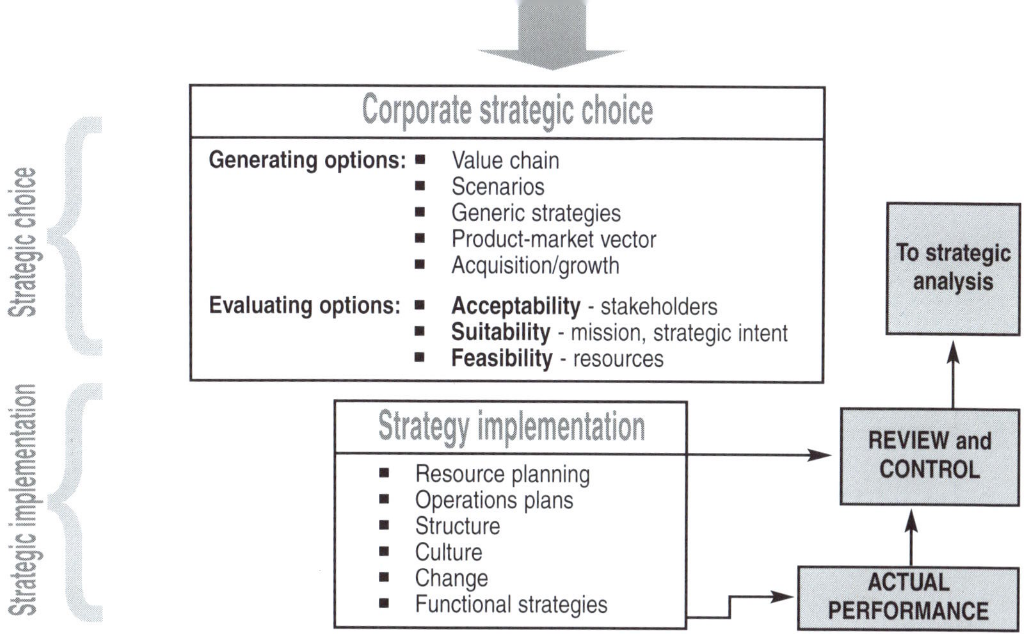
Strategic choice
Strategic implementation
Corporate strategic choice
Generating options:
Value chain
Scenarios
Generic strategies
Product-market vector
Acquisition/growth
Evaluating options:
Acceptability - stakeholders
Suitability - mission, strategic intent
Feasibility - resources
Strategy implementation
Resource planning
Operations plans
Structure
Culture
Change
Functional strategies
To strategic analysis
REVIEW and CONTROL
ACTUAL PERFORMANCE

FOR AND AGAINST THE RATIONAL MODEL

FOR

- Identifies risks
- Forces managers to think
- Forces decision-making
- Formal targets enable control
- Enforces organisational coherence and co-ordination

AGAINST

- Not proven to bring advantage
- May become over formal and reduce initiative
- Assumes internal politics do not exist
- Assumes managers know everything
- Divorces planning from doing
- Cannot cope with shocks and discontinuities

Emergent strategies

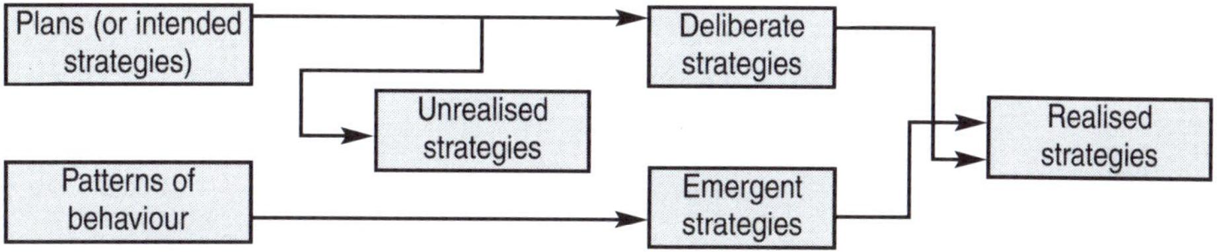

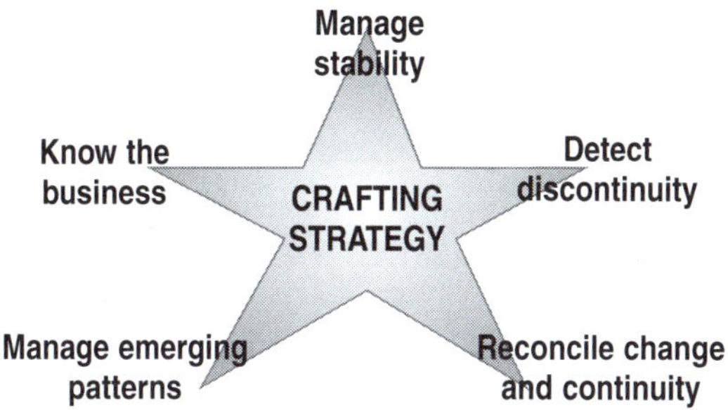

Mintzberg says strategy must be **crafted**

- A purely **deliberate** strategy hampers learning rapidly from experience
- A purely **emergent** strategy hampers control

Bounded rationality

Strategic managers' decision making is constrained by the time and amount of information available to them and by their own skills, habits and awareness.

They:

- Do **not** consider all options, but choose from a restricted range
- Make political compromises by **partisan mutual adjustment**
- **Satisfice** rather than optimise

Incrementalism

Development by small scale extensions of past practices

This approach avoids major errors by the exercise of caution and produces acceptable solutions because it uses consultation, compromise and accommodation.

Logical incrementalism combines this approach with an in-depth review to establish the broad outlines of strategy.

A *learning organisation* puts training and development at the heart of its strategy. It seeks to enhance both its strategic capability and its operations at all levels by continually expanding and utilising knowledge of all kinds. An important aspect is an emphasis on learning by staff at all levels.

Senge suggests 5 essential aspects to the development of the learning organisation.

- **Building a shared vision** focuses everybody's efforts around a single purpose.
- **Personal mastery** by workers at all levels, enhancing their own competence.
- **Mental models** are people's fundamental assumptions about how things should be done. It is necessary that these assumptions be challenged since they hamper fundamental developments.
- **Team learning** must be applied to problems by teams: individual learning is insufficient. Knowledge must be transferred and utilised not hoarded.
- **Systems thinking** tackles problems as wholes rather than breaking them down.

Implications of the learning approach

- Significant innovation can originate anywhere in the organisation
- Organisation structures must respond to opportunities and changed conditions
- Management must create a learning climate and create systems to apply knowledge to problems at all levels.

Notes

Mintzberg

Know the Business

Manage Stability

Detect Discontinuity

Reconcile Change + Continuity

Manage Emerging Patterns.

2: Mission and goals

Topic List

All organisations have a reason for existence. A clear statement of purpose is an important input into management at all levels.

Stakeholders interests are likely to conflict and so they will have differing views about the organisation's strategic plans.

All organisations have a reason for existence. A clear statement of purpose is an important input into management at all levels.

Hamal + Prahalad

Vision

Foresight
Breadth
Uniqueness
Consensus
Actionability

The strategic thinker's idea of what the organisation could be in the future.

It must not ignore practical problems or degenerate into wishful thinking

Strategic intent

A dream, to stretch and energise the organisation, to give a sense of direction and coherence to plans

(*Hamel and Prahalad*)

Mission

'The organisation's basic function in society'

(*Mintzberg*)

Includes, typically:

- Purpose
- Basic strategy eg products
- Policies and standards of behaviour
- Values and culture
  - business principles
  - internal relationships
  - behaviour

A formal **mission statement** may:

- Impress customers
- Motivate staff
- Guide managers actions
- Guide strategic thinking

Direction
Purpose
Values
Place in Market
Nature of Business
Competitive advantage

BUT it may also:

- Be ignored in practice
- Treated cynically as mere PR
- Merely rationalise what is done anyway
- Be the same as everyone else's

Goals and Objectives

Goals and objectives flow from mission. The terminology is not standardised

They should be:

- **S**pecific
- **M**easurable
- **A**ttainable
- **R**esults oriented
- **T**ime bounded

They should balance:

- Long term considerations
- Short term imperatives

They should be **consistent** across the organisation so that all pull together

System goals are self-serving rather than mission-oriented

There is a **hierarchy of objectives**. For a commercial organisation, the highest level of objective will always be based on **profitability** over the long term, though **growth** may be regarded as of equal importance.

Secondary objectives include functional and departmental objectives as well as corporate objectives that support the main objective.

Example

Corporate objective:	Profit improvement
Supporting objectives:	Cut admin costs Improve quality
Despatch dept objective:	Reduce misdeliveries to 3% of total

Conflict between the demands of secondary objectives can be dealt with by:

- **Bargaining** between managers
- **Satisficing** ie satisfactory rather than ideal performance
- **Sequential attention** to goals in turn
- **Priority setting** by senior managers

Stakeholders

Groups or individuals whose interests are directly affected by the organisations activities

Example

Internal	Employees, management
Connected	Owners, suppliers, customers, lenders
External	Government, local communities

Stakeholders' interests are likely to conflict. *Mendelow's* **stakeholder mapping** helps the organisation to establish its priorities and set up its system of corporate governance.

Level of interest

Power	Low (interest)	High (interest)
Low	A	B
High	C	D

A: Minimal effort

B: **Keep informed**; little direct influence but may influence more powerful stakeholders

C: Treat with care; often passive but capable of moving to segment D; **keep satisfied**

D: **Key players** - strategy must be **acceptable** to them, at least

Notes

3: The political context

Topic List

- Political systems
- The democratic process
- Political parties in the UK
- Local and regional government
- The EU

In spite of Labour's continued huge majority in the House of Commons, the political scene in the UK is in a state of flux. The seeming demise of the conservatives, the growth of the Liberal Democrats; our recent adoption of the European Convention on Human Rights and our possible joining of the Euro all mean that we live in interesting times.

Furthermore, virtually all areas of life in the UK are touched by political decisions whether considering health, energy policy, law and order or employment rights. It is therefore, vital that you understand this, the political component of the business context.

Types of political system

Authoritarian

eg North Korea, Iran

- often based on the beliefs of military or religious ethics
- single 'party'
- significant ownership and control by elite
- very restricted civil liberties and extensive censorship
- seeming voting rights but elections often not free or fair
- often very unstable

Communist/ post-communist

eg China, Cuba

- based on the philosophies of Karl Marx
- dominant party but some limited multi party
- significant state ownership and control
- some civil liberties, some censorship
- voting rights and freer and fairer elections
- can be stable or unstable

Liberal Democratic

eg USA, UK

- based to some extent on the work of Adam Smith
- Multiparty
- limited state ownership and control
- robust civil liberties and increasing freedom of information
- universal suffrage and free, fair elections
- mostly stable

These are generalisations. There will always be exceptions and those who disagree, eg Democrats in Florida would not agree that elections in the USA are free and fair!

The UK political system

The UK is a parliamentary democracy with a constitutional monarchy.

Parliament → House of Commons, House of Lords
the decision taking body or executive

Democracy → rule by the people who exercise their right by voting in elections, forming or belonging to political parties or forming or belonging to pressure groups

Constitutional → unlike many other liberal democracies the UK does not have a definitive written constitution. Our constitution is enshrined in common law, past practice and most recently the (European Convention on) Human Rights Act 1998

Monarchy → today mostly titular with restricted power

Note also the judiciary (law enforcement) that can constrain Parliament via the High Court, the ECJ and the European Court of Human Rights

The role of political parties and pressure groups

The public

join political parties

↓

raise issues of concern

↓

issues discussed at annual party conference

↓

manifesto formed and put to ...

↓

The public

→ who vote for their candidate of choice

↑

party members and MPs vote for a party leader

↑

the monarch asks the majority party leader to form a government

↑

the party leader becomes PM

↑

the PM appoints the cabinet to form the government

→ the government initiate legislation

↓

Parliament enacts

↓

The Monarch assents

Pressure groups differ from political parties. they are concerned with single issues rather that the full range of social and economic policy, eg Greenpeace.

Ideas associated with the UK's three main parties

Conservatives

- durable social order
- free market and competition
- low state intervention
- monetarism
- low taxation
- low government expenditure
- sterling
- Euro-scepticism

Labour

- socialism
- repudiation of class
- redistribution of wealth
- public ownership

New Labour

- abandoned commitment to public ownership
- democratic socialism
- public/private partnership
- fair competition
- the '3rd way'
- divided over Europe

Liberal Democrats

- formed from the SDP and Liberals in 1981
- fair, free, open society
- balance between liberty, equality and community
- environmentally sustainable growth
- proportional representation
- pro-Europe

Is the UK a two or three party system? Some claim the Conservatives are in terminal decline, the Liberal Democrats are growing. Which can claim to be the loyal opposition?

'Local authorities' are elected bodies with limited autonomy and authority over a specific geographical area. They resolve local conflicts and administer policy as established by central government. They raise revenue via the council tax

Power

Tends to be proportionate to size. Thus District Councils have limited power while County and Metropolitan County Councils have far more.

The recently established devolved, regional governments of Wales and Scotland have still more power, although still with some control from Central Government.

Elections

- Councillors mostly serve a 4-year fixed term. Voter turn-out is poor, often less than 50%.

Relationships with Central Government

- Historically have been quite turbulent, especially with the Metropolitan County Councils

The Future

- A further shift towards local autonomy and English Regional Government as proposed for North East England. Will this be useful or just another layer of government?

The main bodies/institutions

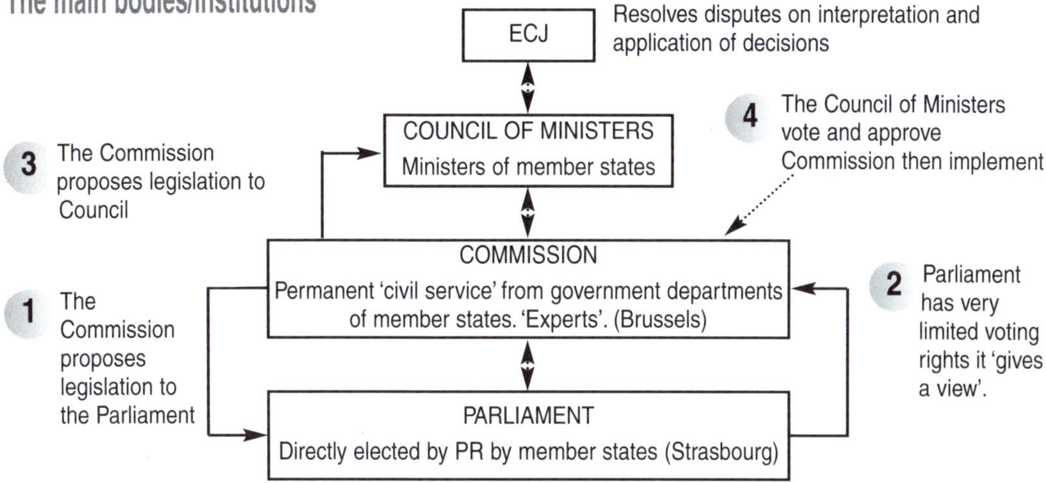

Decisions of the EU

These come in the form of:

Treaties → The fundamental philosophies and rules of the union, eg Treaty of Rome (1957). Binding on all member states although some limited opt-out by agreement eg UK at Maastricht (1991)

Regulations → These are automatically binding on all member states, eg EC Social Security Regulations 1986

Directives → These are implemented by member states via their own legislative processes and machinery
eg UK Working Time Regulations 1998, came into force as a result of the Working TIme Directive UK: Parental Leave Regulations introduced by the Employment Regulations Act 1999, came into force as a result of the Parental Leave Directive.

4: The economic context

Changes in the external environment mean that managers have to develop and adapt strategy in order that their organisations can survive and remain competitive. The PESTLE/E (Political, Economic, Social, Technological, Legal, Environmental, Ethical) influences are subject to constant change. Managers of private, public and voluntary sectors will seek to minimise threats to the business and maximise opportunities when disturbances occur.

Governments will seek to control the economy in a variety of ways in order to achieve a range of objectives, such as economic growth, low inflation, high levels of unemployment and to manage the balance of payments. International trade, in general and the effects of globalisation, in particular have a significant impact on all types of organisations.

Topic List

Public sector

Activities undertaken by government including defence, justice, security, health and education; and businesses owned by government, ie nationalised industries.

Private sector

Includes not-for-profit organisations such as charities and profit making businesses. Sole traders and partners have **unlimited liability**. Shareholders in companies or corporations do not. Incorporated businesses may be divided into those that may offer shares to the public (UK plc) and those that may not (UK Ltd).

Primary sector Produces raw materials: agriculture, forestry, mining, oil and gas production

Secondary sector Manufacture of goods; construction; energy; water

Tertiary sector Provides services, including distribution, catering and public services

As they grow, national economies tend to develop from having a dominant primary sector to having a much more important secondary sector and eventually to consisting largely of the tertiary sector.

Economics is concerned with the production and consumption of goods and services: what to produce, how to produce it and who to produce it for.

Scarcity of resources

The production of goods and services requires the utilisation of economic **resources**. These resources are **scarce** and therefore choices must be made to how they are to be employed.

- LAND includes all **natural resources**. Land itself is limited in quantity but can be improved in quality.
- LABOUR is people employed to produce goods and services. It varies in quality.
- CAPITAL consists of physical goods that aid production. Money can be transformed into real capital.
- ENTERPRISE is needed both to organise production and to take the risk of possible financial loss.

Factor rewards

Land is rewarded with **rent**. **Labour** is rewarded with **wages**. **Capital** is rewarded with **interest**. **Enterprise** is rewarded with **profit**

Economic growth

Economic welfare

Economic welfare is primarily determined by two things.

- The level of output of goods and services
- The existence of negative externalities such as pollution, noise and social dislocation

The distribution of output among the population is also an economic welfare issue.

Factors influencing growth

Economic growth depends on the quality and quantity of scarce resources available and the efficiency with which they are used. Technological advances; education and training; and increases in either the population or the participation rate all lead to growth.

Sustainable growth

Economic growth that exceeds the rate of population growth leads to a generally higher standard of living. However, there are problems with economic growth:

- Depletion of natural resources: are substitutes available?
- Negative externalities reduce the rate of growth of economic welfare, since they must be borne or resource used to limit their effects.
- Growth brings human problems such as unemployment.

A market

Potential buyers and potential sellers come together for the purpose of exchange.

Sellers are **firms**. Buyers of consumers goods are **households**.

Consumers are rational

- They prefer more to less.
- They will substitute one good for another if the price is right.
- They attempt to maximise satisfaction from a limited income.
- Satisfaction diminishes as consumption increases.

The demand curve

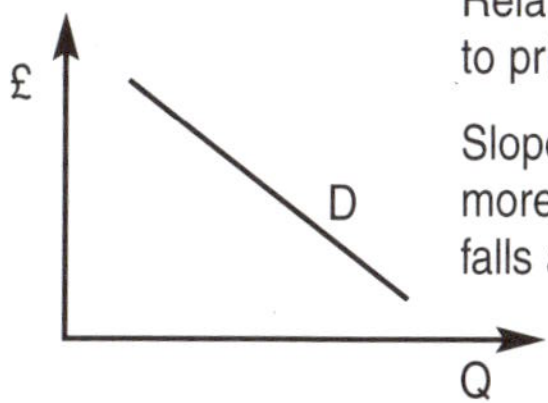

Relates quantity demanded to price payable

Slopes down because more demanded as price falls and vice versa

Demand is also influenced by

- Price of other goods
- Income
- Taste and fashion
- Expectation of price changes

Substitutes

are goods that are alternatives (eg tea and coffee). A rise in the price of a good is likely to produce an **increase** in demand for its substitutes.

Complements

are goods that are bought and used together (eg tea and milk). A rise in the price of a good is likely to produce a **fall** in demand for its complement.

- If demand for a good rises when household income rises, it is a **normal good** (eg steak). If demand falls, it is an **inferior good** (eg mince).

The supply curve

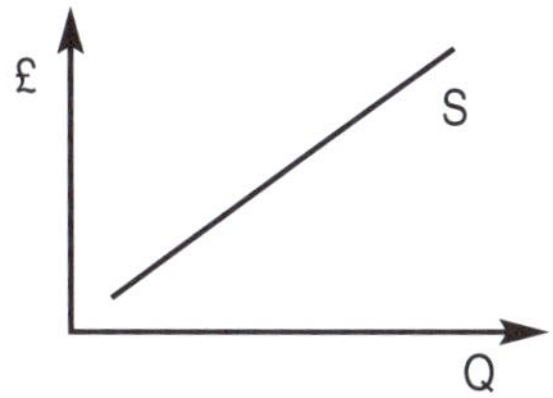

Relates quantity offered to price available.

Just as with demand, the effect of other factors is to cause a shift in the position of the demand curve.

Factors influencing supply

A shift of the supply curve to the right could be caused by any of the factors below.

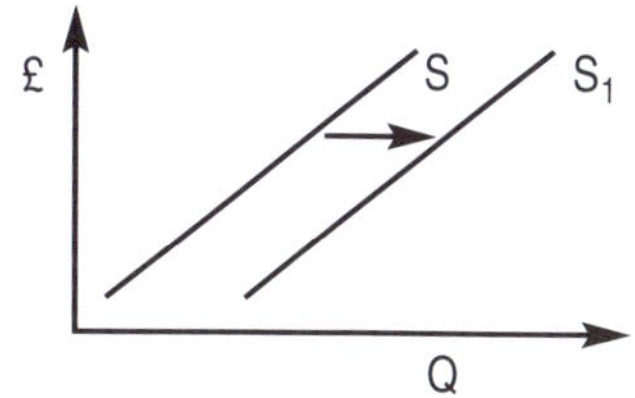

- Expectation of a future fall in price, to obtain a better price now
- A fall in the price of a **substitute in supply** — A good that can be produced using the same resources
- A rise in the price of a **good in joint supply** — Goods in joint supply are unavoidably produced together (eg hides and meat).
- Technological improvements
- Factors that reduce output directly (eg industrial disruption, natural disasters, bad weather, political disturbances

The opposite effects will move the curve to the left.

The price mechanism

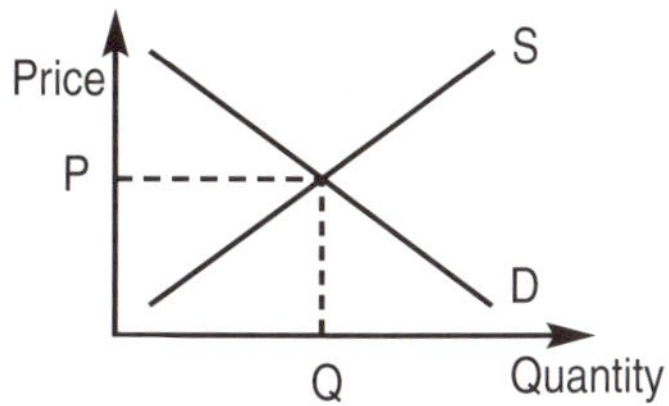

The price mechanism brings supply and demand together at the **equilibrium price** P. This is also the **market clearing price** since quantity Q is both offered and demanded and there is neither surplus nor shortage.

Functions of the price mechanism

- Market prices and their movements act as **signals** to producers, enabling them to produce what is most needed.
- When a firm operates efficiently, responding to market signals and controlling its costs, it receives a **reward** in the form of profit.
- The actions of firms in responding to the profit opportunities **allocate** resources to their best use.

Governments intervene in microeconomic matters when market forces do not produce the outcomes they wish to see. The various aspects of **market failure** invite government regulation. The extreme form of intervention is **nationalisation** and this may be undertaken for other reasons.

Government response to market failure

- **Monopoly elements** – controls on prices or profits - breaking up monopoly companies ('trust busting')
- **Externalities** – regulations (eg to control pollution, compel car insurance, ban smoking)
- **Imperfect information** – product safety rules, public service advertising, provision of jobcentres

Other justifications for nationalisation

- **Natural monopolies** should not be allowed to exploit their position (eg utilities companies)
- Larger groupings could exploit further economies of scale to natural advantage (eg aerospace)
- Only government can supply enough finance for some industries (eg railway networks)
- Political control over strategic industries (eg oil production)
- Marxist/socialist theory. The political left is more or less uncomfortable with capitalism and wishes to control industry for the benefit of its client groups (eg coal mining)

Western governments promote competition in most areas of economic activity since it is a simple and cheap way to achieve economic efficiency and growth.

The UK Competition Commission

The CC may investigate when one firm controls 25% of the market or when a merger involves more than £75m of assets worldwide. It reports to the government. It seeks to promote consumer interests, competition, enterprise and efficiency and tries to balance rewards for innovation and the benefits of scale economies against the disadvantages of monopoly.

There has been a move away from government control of industry in the West over the last 20 years.

Reasons for reducing the degree of government control

- Nationalised industries being run for the convenience of their staffs rather than their customers
- Civil servants and politicians not good at commercial decision making
- Sale of state assets permits tax cuts and reduces need for government borrowing
- Enhanced competition seen as likely to improve efficiency and promote growth
- Reduction in enforcement costs and unintended consequences of regulation
- Wider share ownership

Privatisation

It is possible to discern several strands in privatisation.

- **Deregulation**, to allow private firms to compete with state-owned ones (eg postal services)
- **Contracting out** of government work previously done by government employees (eg waste collection)
- **Outright sale** of businesses to private shareholders (eg British Telecom)

Privatisation has been criticised

- Creation of private monopolies
- Sale of assets at a discount
- Enhanced top executive benefits
- Decline in quantity and quality of service

Economic Growth

A country's national income is the value of the economic wealth its people create in a year by undertaking economic activity, that is, by providing goods and services.

The measurement national income is subject to conventions and errors of measurement

- Work done by people for themselves is not included, nor is barter trade
- The size of the undeclared or 'black' economy is, by definition, unknown
- Government services are included at cost; commercially provided services valuation includes an element of profit

Why calculate national income?

- Assist government economic planning
- Permit international comparison
- Measure standard of living

Standard of living is normally expressed in terms of national income per head of population. This is useful for establishing trends but must be used with care for international comparisons.

The circular flow of income in the economy has a real existence which is reflected by money flows.

Firms produce goods and services that are consumed by households and receive money payment.

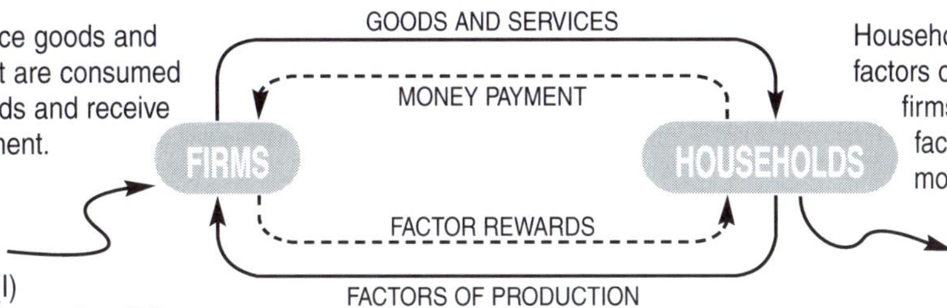

Households provide the factors of production that firms need and receive factor rewards in money form.

Injections
Investment (I)
Government spending (G)
Exports (X)

Withdrawals
Savings (S)
Taxation (T)
Imports (I)

GDP	+	Net property income from abroad	=	GNP	–	Capital consumption	=	National income
(The value of the goods and services produced by the economy in one year)		(income from abroad less payments made)				(depreciation of capital assets)		

Disadvantages of inflation

- Redistribution of income and wealth from creditors to debtors since debts' real value diminishes
- Impoverishment of those on fixed incomes
- Resource costs of changing prices, eg issue of new price lists
- Reduction in growth of GDP due to uncertainty about costs and in extreme cases (hyperinflation) reluctance to use the currency

Causes of inflation

- **Demand pull** inflation arises when Aggregate Demand is greater than the economy's productive capacity (ie inflationary gap).
- **Cost push** inflation can occur when costs of factors of production increase even though they are not in short supply. This is particularly apparent in the case of **labour**; strong trade unions can drive up wages even when the economy is underproducing. Import costs are also an important source of inflation.
- **Expectations** of inflation can actually bring it about, when they lead to increased wage demands.

Measuring inflation in the UK

RPI is an index of a wide rage of costs.

RPIX excludes mortgage payments from the index.

Categories of unemployment

- **Frictional**: time is required to match job seekers with available vacancies. The unemployment is short-term.
- **Seasonal** unemployment is typical of some industries, such as agriculture and tourism.
- **Structural**: long term changes in an industry reduce the demand for labour. This may be the result of long term decline or technology-based productivity improvements.
- **Cyclical** or **demand deficient**: during the downswing of the trade cycle, demand contracts and there is a deflationary gap. Output and employment both fall.

Consequences of unemployment

- Loss of output
- Loss of 'human capital', ie skills
- Increasing income inequalities
- Social costs such as mental health problems, divorce and crime
- Effect on government finances of increased welfare payments

Calculating unemployment

$$\frac{\text{Number unemployed}}{\text{Total workforce}} \times 100\%$$

Both quantities are subject to statistical errors and political massage.

Multinational companies (MNCs)

operate in more than one country, rather than just trading internationally. Ownership or control of a production or service facility in another country is the test. Major MNCs such as Ford have turnover greater than the GNP of small countries.

International trade

is regulated by a complex system of bilateral, multilateral, regional and global agreements. The World Trade Organisation promotes global agreements.

MNCs and globalisation of trade

Reasons for multinational operations

- **Cost advantage**: reduce cost of transport to final market by manufacturing locally; exploit availability of cheap labour
- **Expand by horizontal integration**: access markets protected by tariffs; seek economies of scale from increased turnover
- **Local market requirements**: satisfy by local manufacturing and distribution

Global financial markets

Improved IT systems and deregulation of markets mean capital can be moved rapidly around the world in order to achieve the best returns.

MNCs and the national economy

- MNCs may import **capital**, thus expanding potential GNP. Even where local capital is used, they may mobilise it better
- MNCs may **transfer technology**, again expanding potential GNP
- MNCs will bring advanced **management practices** and **IT systems**
- MNCs may exploit different tax systems, using **transfer pricing** to declare profits in countries where they pay least tax
- **Remission of profits** out of the country is a withdrawal from the circular flow
- MNCs may require **subsidies** or **tax privileges** before establishing operations

Arguments for protection of international trade

- **Employment protection**: cheap imports from low wage countries mean domestic industries cannot compete. Business failure and unemployment ensue.
- **Balance of payments**: imports must be financed or the exchange rate will be driven down. Restricting imports reduces the pressure.
- **Infant industries**: less developed countries need to assist their developing industries to become established.
- **Unfair trade practices**: exporters may sell at less than cost ('dumping') to gain a foothold; governments may subsidise exports.
- **Revenue**: tariffs raise revenue painlessly.
- **Strategic industries**: some industries (defence, agriculture) are favoured for strategic reasons.

Arguments against protection of international trade

- **Reduction in welfare**: protection reduces global trade and hence global production.
- **Inefficiency**: domestic industries become inefficient through lack of competition. Also, declining industries linger and new ones are hampered.
- **Higher prices**: cheap imports reduce the cost of living.
- **Retaliation**: retaliatory response by other countries is likely to harm the domestic economy.

European Union

The European Union (EU) combines a free trade area with a customs union and a common market. The aim is complete freedom of trade, including free movement of capital and labour and no national preference in the award of public sector contracts. However, barriers still exist in the form of different tax systems, infrastructure, skill levels and prosperity.

The **European Economic Area** links the EU to Norway and Iceland.

North American Free Trade Agreement

The North American Free Trade Agreement links Mexico, the USA and Canada in a free trade area.

Aims of World Trade Organisation

- Reduce barriers to free trade
- Eliminate discrimination in trade
- Deter protectionist measures

Free trade area: no restrictions on the supply of goods and services.

Customs union: a free trade area with common external tariffs on imports from non-member countries.

Common market: a customs union with free movement of factors of production: this may lead to harmonisation of economic policy, taxation and commercial law; and political co-operation.

A country's balance of payments is a statement of the value of its transactions with other countries.

UK balance of payments 1999 (net amounts)

	£bn
Current account	
Trade in goods	–26,767
Trade in services	11,538
Income	8,332
Transfers	–4,084
Current balance	–10,981
Capital account	776
Financial account	5,853
Net errors and omissions	4,352
	0

- Trade in goods: Used to be called 'visible trade'
- Income: Profits, dividends, interest, wages and salaries
- Transfers: Includes foreign aid, payments to EU and UN and individual deposits
- Capital account: Movement in fixed assets
- Financial account: Transfer of ownership of businesses, bonds and shares
- Net errors and omissions: Samples are used rather than 100% record of transactions
- Trade in goods / Trade in services: The UK always imports more goods than it sells overseas, but normally has a surplus on services.
- Total (0): The balance of payments is a double entry system: it must sum to zero.

5: The social context

Topic List

Demographic trends

The workforce

Ethnicity

This chapter covers the change in society and demographic trends. Although these changes tend to be over a long period of time organisations need to respond accordingly.

The population of the UK in 1996 was 58.8 million with a projection of 62.2 million in 2021.

The size and structure of the population has implications for an organisation in terms of workforce size and composition and the demand for its goods or services.

The general trends are that birth rates will continue to fall and life expectancy to rise. These trends have resulted in an aging population in UK and most of Europe.

The working population is fairly stable at 28.5 million but there have been significant changes in its structure.

Example

In 1997 the women comprised 45% of the workforce. Working patterns changed to accommodate this growing section of the workforce (part-time, term time only, flexi-time etc). The demand for goods and services has also been influenced by womens' increased economic participation

Example

The UK workforce is aging. This has significant implications for firms in terms of recruitment and selection and funding of pensions.

Example

Falling birth rates and the increased participation in post comprehensive education has resulted in a reduced number of young people entering the workforce. This has had a significant impact on recruitment and selection and particularly training and development.

Class

Post industrial UK has seen the numbers of working class manual workers decline.

At the same time the middle class has increased due to the growth in jobs in technology and new professions.

Gender

Although the numbers of women in the workforce have grown substantially there are still areas where significant inequality exists.

Women are more likely to work part-time than men. There are more women at the lower levels of organisations.

Example

Women work predominantly in the following main areas of employment.

Clerical and administration
Teaching, nursing and social work
Retailing and catering
Hair dressing and cleaning

These are traditionally low paid areas of work. Even in these areas where women outnumber men they are still not equally represented at senior management level.

Ethnicity

Modern day migration to the UK began in 1945 when immigrants arrived from the former colonies.

The groups vary in many ways, for example, economic activity and educational achievement.

The Race Relations Act 1976 outlawed discrimination on the grounds of race and the Commission for Racial Equality was set up to foster improved race relations.

The 1991 census asked people to classify their ethnic group of which there were eight

- White
- Black-Caribbean
- Black-other
- Indian
- Pakistan
- Bangladesh
- Chinese
- Any other ethnic group

Organisations must ensure all ethnic groups are treated equally, for example, when recruiting. selecting, training and promoting.

Today the demand for goods and services reflects the UK's multi-cultural society.

Notes

6: The technological context

Topic List

- ICT/ IT
- Impact on organisations

Technology had long has an impact on organisations and the people who work in them. In recent times the speed of change and thus the impact has gathered pace. New developments in materials, processes, equipment and particularly information technology have meant that businesses need to be aware of and ideally ahead of technological developments.

IT (Information Technology) is increasingly referred to as ICT (Information and Communication Technology). The growth on the use of ICT in the 1990's has resulted in a revolution in organisation's communications networks both internally (intranets) and externally (internet).

The effect of ICT has not only been felt in the organsiation's communications but in the fundamental way that people work. Management, co-ordination and production work have all been radically changed.

Example

The explosion in ICT/IT has meant that work is no longer constrained by time and /or location. Mobile phones, video conferencing, email and a range of other tools and techniques have enabled some workers to work effectively away from the office.

Example

Many labour intensive processes have now become capital intensive with the introduction of CAD (computer assisted design) and CAM (computer aided manufacturing). This has had an impact on employment in the manufacturing sector in particular.

Example

ICT means that organisations can more effectively integrate all work. Speedy effective links between customers and suppliers can be established. Many organsiations are developing electronic markets in which to sell their products. services.

Example

Technology enables organsiations to compete in gloabal markets. However the growth of the ICT/ IT has also opened up the domestic market to global competition.

7: The legal context

Topic List

The beginning of the 21st century sees the continued trend to seek legal redress for alleged wrongful acts. Nowhere is this more evident than in the area of employment law. To operate effectively and safely, todays' HR practitioner must understand how law is made in the UK and how the English Courts and tribunals operate.

Contract law is at the heart of the employment relationship, but this is increasingly supplemented by statute law, much of it originating in the EU. The UK has been at the forefront in developing anti-discrimination legislation which is increasingly important in a diverse workforce. Termination of employment is another area covered by extensive controls and where the penalties for non-compliance can be severe.

Criminal liability

A **crime** is conduct prohibited by law. Crimes are punishable, usually by fine or imprisonment.

The state prosecutes. It must prove **beyond reasonable doubt** that the accused committed the crime.

Civil liability

Civil law exists to regulate disputes over the rights and obligations of persons dealing with each other.

- Prove on **balance of probabilities**
- Between claimant and defendant
- Key area for businesses is **contract**

Distinction

The distinction is not the act but the legal consequences.

Example

A drunk driver colliding with a pedestrian may create both a civil and a criminal action.

Criminal Prosecution by the State for driving with excess alcohol.

Civil Pedestrian sues for compensation for personal injury.

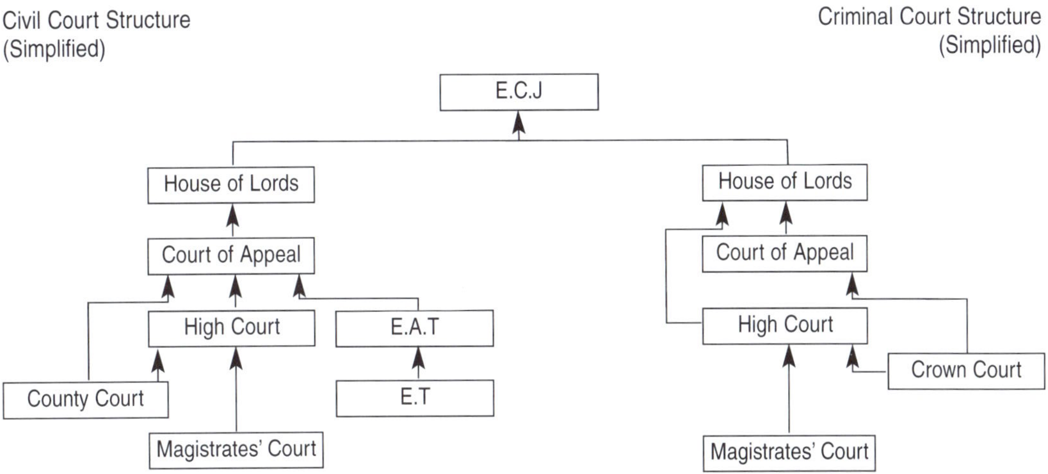

The role of each court and their relationship with each other is shown below.

Status of courts

Function	Appeals to	Bound by	Binds
Magistrates court			
Tries minor crimes summarily Committals to crown court	Crown court	High court Court of Appeal	No one Not even itself
Limited family and other civil jurisdiction	High court	House of Lords ECJ	
County court			
Majority of civil cases in UK (Contract & tort < £25,000, equitable matters, land < £30,000, undefended matrimonial, probate < £30,000, some bankruptcy, small claims < £5,000)	High court	High court Court of Appeal House of Lords ECJ	No one Not even itself
Crown court			
All indictable crimes with a jury	Court of Appeal (criminal)	High court (QBD) Court of Appeal	No one (However, cases are persuasive)
Limited civil cases (appeals from magistrates court on licensing/betting)	High court (QBD)	House of Lords ECJ	

Case law and judicial precedent

Status of courts

Function	Appeals to	Bound by	Binds
Employment Tribunal			
Hears applications under employment law, including unfair dismissal, pay and discrimination	Employment Appeal Tribunal	EAT Court of Appeal and House of Lords ECJ (on EU law only)	No one Not even itself
Employment Appeal Tribunal			
Hears appeals on points of law only from the ET	Court of Appeal ECJ	Court of Appeal and House of Lords ECJ (on EU law only)	ET

Case law

The basis of case law is that the law is interpreted by the courts and evolves with cases being tried.

A court's decision is expected to be consistent with previous decisions. Therefore there has to be access to decisions made previously in the courts. This is contained in **law reports**.

The doctrine of judicial precedent

is based on the view that a function of the judge is to decide cases in accordance with existing case law. It provides consistency in the law. A judge must follow precedents set according to certain rules.

Rules

- A precedent must be based on a **proposition of law**, not a decision on a question of fact
- It must form part of the **ratio decidendi** of the case, that is, the judge's reason for deciding
- The **material facts** of each case must be the same
- The **status** of the previous court must be such that it binds the court seeking precedent
- A judge may make statements 'by the way', ie, not part of the ratio. These are **obiter dicta**

Legislation

or statute, is law made by Parliament. Parliament can make new law, repeal old law, overrule old law and enact law as directed by the EU. This is known as 'Parliamentary sovereignty'.

Parliamentary procedure

- Proposal aired in a Green Paper
- Comments incorporated into a White Paper, setting out aims
- Legislation put forward as draft Bill
- Bill passes through Commons and Lords (First reading, second reading, committee stage, report stage, third reading)
- Royal Assent

Delegated legislation means rules of law made by other subordinate bodies eg local authorities have the power to make Bye-laws. This saves parliamentary time but lacks parliamentary accountability.

EU Law:

- Treaty of Rome 1957
- Treaty of Amsterdam 1997
- Treaty of Nice 2001

Some articles of the Treaty of Rome have direct effect

Three **secondary sources** of law:

Direct applicability

means that the law comes into force in member states without the member states passing domestic law.

Direct effect

means that law confers rights and imposes obligations directly on individuals.

Regulations

Directly applicable

Generally restricted to matters within the basic aims of the Treaty of Rome, eg establishment of a single market, so law against anti-competitive practices.

Directives

Issued to member state governments, giving a period of time to incorporate the principles into domestic law.

Example: Working Time Directive 1995

Decisions

These are administrative in nature, from the EC.

Addressed to a state, person or company.

Has a direct effect on the recipient.

The contract of employment

At the heart of the employment relationship its formation is governed by the general law of contract but it is also increasingly impacted by employment law enacted by statute.

This section examines this complex area of the law under the following headings:

- What is a contract?
- Employees and independent contractors
- Sources of the terms of the employment contract
- Changing the terms
- Breach of contract
- Discharge

Lastly, the crucially important concept of the psychological contract is considered. It must be remembered that this is **NOT** legally binding or enforceable in law.

What is a contract?

It is defined as an agreement that is legally binding. It can be oral or written and parties are judged by what they have said, written or done.

Three essential elements

- Agreement by offer and acceptance
- Intention to create legal relations
- Consideration: a mutual exchange of value, eg work in exchange for pay.

Factors that might affect the validity of the contract

- Capacity, eg minors
- Form, some contracts must follow a particular form, eg credit sales.
- Content, there may be both express and implied terms
- Genuine consent, there may be undue duress or misrepresentation due to a mistake
- Legality, the courts will not enforce a contract that is illegal or contrary to public policy.

Privity of contract. Only a person who is a party to a contract has enforceable rights or obligations in it. Third parties have a right of action in exceptional circumstances.

It is important to distinguish between employees and independent contractors. The courts will look at the reality of the situation and then apply three tests.

Reality of the situation

What the parties say is less conclusive than the reality of the situation.

If there is doubt as to the nature of the relationship, the courts will look at the agreement between the parties.

Tests applied by the courts

Control test: Has the employer control over the way in which the employee performs his duties?

Mutual obligation test: If the employee is so skilled that he cannot be controlled, is he integrated into the organisation?

Multiple (economic reality) test: Is the employee really working on his own account?

Case box

Ferguson v John Dawson & Partners 1976

Massey v Crown Life Assurance 1978

Motorola v Davidson (1) and Melville Group (2) 2000

Carmichael & Leese v National Power Plc (2000)

Ready Mixed Concrete (South East) v Ministry of Pensions & NI 1968

Significant factors

Does the employee use his own **tools and equipment,** or does the employer provide? Does the 'employer' have the right to **choose and dismiss employees**? If **salary** is paid this is a fair indication that the individual is an employee. Working for a number of **different people** is not necessarily a sign of self-employment **neither is just the 'labels' the parties use to describe their relationship.**

Importance of distinction

Factor	Employee	Independent contractor
Tax/social security	Class 1 NI ('ers and 'ees) Deductions under PAYE (Sch E)	IC pays Class 2 and 4 Report to IR on Sch D
Legal protection	Substantial employment law	Less protection
Contractual rights	Number of rights and duties are implied into contract of employment	Rights and duties do not extend to a contract for services
Bankruptcy	Employee has preferential rights as a creditor	IC would be a standard creditor, therefore get paid later
Health and Safety	There is significant common law and statutory protection	In practice the protection extends to ICs and employees
VAT	Irrelevant in capacity as 'ee	May need to register for sales

An employment contract may contain

- **Express terms** - Those which are clearly set out as agreed by the parties, (normally and advisedly in writing)
- **Implied terms** - Those which are not expressly included. Most implied terms are present by virtue of common law.

  eg Employer's duty of care and to pay wages
  Employees duty to obey reasonable orders
  Mutual duty of trust and confidence
- **Incorporated terms** - Those agreed by collective agreement
  - Those specified by statue, eg, Equal Pay Act 1970
- **Implied by custom and practice** - Where actual behaviours and practices supersede specified contractual terms.

NOTE: The employee can always rely on the most advantageous term in the contract.

Terms of an employment contract

A contract of employment sets out the scope and limitations of duties and rights and obligations of both employer and employee.

Whether written or oral, under the Employment Rights Act 1996, some written particulars must be given to employees within two months of commencement of employment.

The statement is not the contract itself. This is created when the job offer is made and accepted. The statement of particulars is the employers' view of these terms.

The statement of written particulars must include:

- Name of the employer and employee
- The date on which employment began
- Details relating to continuous service
- Pay, scale or rate and intervals of payment
- Hours of work/ normal working hours
- Holidays and public holidays
- Holiday pay
- Sick leave and sick leave entitlement *
- Pensions and pension schemes *
- Length of notice of termination to be given on each side.
- Job title or brief job description
- Disciplinary and grievance rules *

* May refer to separate documents

Changing a contract

The extent to which it is possible to change or vary terms is dependent on how the contract was formed in the first place. Employers can build in some flexibility allowing them to make reasonable changes, eg to location. In this case there is no variation and changes in location are lawful.

- **Variation by mutual agreement**
- **Variation by collective agreement**
  Where changes to a collective agreement may incorporate changed terms into individual contract.
- **Variation by failure to reject changes**
  Where an employer applies new terms that the employee finds unsatisfactory but nevertheless continues to work under the new terms without protest. After a short time this could be deemed to have constituted acceptance.
- **Variation by prior notice**
  Where an employer gives advance notice of changes. As above, if not overtly rejected this could be deemed acceptance.
- **Variation by termination and re-employment**
  Where revised contract terms are rejected by the employee, the employer may dismiss by notice. The employer can re-appoint on the new terms. The dismissed employee may complain to an ET.

Breach of contract

If an employer attempts to impose a variation of contract on an employee without agreement, this will normally be a breach of contract. Employees can:

Acquiesce

ie do nothing and work to the new contract. After a short time they will be deemed to have implicitly accepted the breach.

Sue for breach of contract

ie pursue a claim for damages (financial loss) in the County Court.

If they consider the breach a fundamental one, they could resign and claim constructive dismissal (and possibly damages on termination) in the Employment Tribunal.

Discharge of contract

There are a variety of ways in which a contract may be discharged, including when one is breached as detailed above.

Methods of discharge

- Performance - This is the normal method of discharge
- Frustration - When some outside event makes the contract incapable of performance

NOTE: Fixed-term contracts that run to end of the agreed term are discharged by performance.

The psychological contract

Although important in securing the employment contract, the psychological contract is **NOT ENFORCEABLE IN LAW** and there are no remedies for breach via the courts or Tribunal

The psychological contract pertains to mutual expectations rather than mutual obligations
eg the employee's expectation to be stimulated and challenged by the role
the employer's expectation that the employee will be flexible and responsive to change.

Failure of the psychological contract is likely to lead to the employee seeking alternative employment. The employer may seek solution by offering training support and/or taking disciplinary action.

See also 'Managing People' Motivation Theory

Equal opportunities and anti-discrimination legislation

Anti-discrimination legislation seeks to promote fairness and equality and provides the background for equal opportunities policies. It is a critical element in managing the employment relationship effectively, beginning with recruitment/ selection right through to termination of contract. In the areas of sex, race and disability discrimination job applicants, not just employees, may make claims to the Employment Tribunal.

Areas covered by legislation:

- Sex or marital status
- Parental leave
- Part-time status
- Equal pay
- Race (including ethnicity, colour and nationality)
- Sexual orientation
- Disability
- Rehabilitation of offenders
- Trade union membership/ non-membership
- Asylum and immigration
- Religion and belief

NOTE: it is proposed to introduce anti-discrimination legislation to cover age (2006).

Sex discrimination Act 1975/ Race Relations Act 1976

These two statues are similar in a number of ways

- Both set up commissions to enforce the acts

  - the CRE, Commission for Racial Equality
  - the EOC, Equal Opportunities Commission

- Both statues declare discrimination **unlawful** and racial or sexual harassment may constitute a criminal offence that can result in imprisonment.

- The key elements of both acts are
  - direct/indirect discrimination
  - genuine occupational qualification (GOQ)
  - positive action

NOTE: The Race Relations Amendment Act applies additional conditions on public sector employers

Key elements

- Direct discrimination is where a person is treated less favourably on the grounds of their sex or race
- Indirect discrimination occurs where a condition is applied that disadvantages a higher proportion of one sex or race
- A GOQ allows an employer to employ or promote someone of a specific sex or race because of the requirements of the job.
- Positive action, ie the encouragement of persons from under-represented groups, is lawful.

Parental leave

Employment Act 2002

Under the terms of this legislation new rights for working parents were introduced.

- Paternity leave and pay (Dec 2002)
- Adoption leave and pay (Dec 2002)
- Enhanced maternity leave and pay (April 2003)
- Rights to work flexibly for parents with children under the age of six.

The employer is required to give serious consideration to applications to work flexibly.

In effect this will be an application to vary the contract and can apply to hours of work, times of work and location.

Part time status

Part-time workers (prevention of less favourable treatment) Regulations 2000

These regulations came into effect in July 2000 under the Employment Relations Act 1999, giving effect to the EU Part-time Workers Directive.

- Part time workers are given the right not to be treated less favourably than full-time workers.
- The regulations cover:
  pay and overtime pay
  sickness and maternity pay
  holiday
  pensions
  maternity and parental leave
- In general terms, the provisions should apply pro rata.

Equal Pay

Equal Pay Act, 1970

- For: 'Like' or 'similar' work or where work is rated 'equivalent' under a job evaluation scheme
- 1983 Amendment introduced equal pay for work of equal value
- Employers can defend pay inequalities if there is a 'Genuine Material Factor' (GMF) eg based on difference in performance or productivity, length of employment, experience, skills or competency or market conditions.

NOTE also Minimum Wage Act, 1998

Disability

Disability Discrimination Act, 1995

- It is unlawful to discriminate against a disabled person for a reason that relates to that disability
- 'Disability' is defined as a physical or mental impairment that has a substantial and long-term (12 months or more),adverse effect of a person's ability to carry out normal day to day activities.
- Companies employing fewer than 15 employees are exempt.
- Does not distinguish between 'direct' and 'indirect' discrimination, instead it cites 'less favourable treatment' unless the employer can make a 'reasonable adjustment'
- Requires employers to make 'reasonable adjustments' to meet individual needs eg physical adjustments to buildings or to working arrangements.

Rehabilitation of offenders

Rehabilitation of Offenders Act 1974

- it is unlawful to discriminate against someone with 'spent' convictions
- Custodial sentences of more than $2\frac{1}{2}$ years are never spent
- Note also Criminal Records Bureaux (Police Act, 1997)

Trade union membership/ non membership

Employment Relations Act 1999

- Unlawful to discriminate on grounds of trade union membership or non membership or activities
- Unlawful to 'blacklist' TU members
- TU officials are given special protection

Religion

- Special rules in Northern Ireland
- From December 2003 unlawful to discriminate on the basis of religion or belief in the rest of UK.

Asylum and immigration

Asylum & Immigration Act 1996 &1999

- A CRIMINAL offense to 'knowingly' or 'recklessly' employ someone not allowed to work in the UK
- Maximum fine currently £5,000
- Employers must verify that ALL applicants qualify

Health and safety

General issues

Businesses in the UK owe a care of duty in respect of health and safety to:

- their employees
- members of the public affected by their employees
- other peoples employees working on their premises, eg contractors
- members of the public, eg passers by and customers

In most cases a civil liability will arise, in many so too will a criminal liability

Employers have vicarious liability for the actions of their employees.

Under common law the employer has a duty to provide:

- a safe place to work and means of access
- a safe system of work (see also H&S at W Act,1974)
- safe equipment and materials
- competent work fellows
- protection from the risk of injury

Health and Safety at Work Act, 1974

This repeats the common law listed above. In addition the Act :

- Set up the H&S Executive and H&S Commission
- Established HSE Inspectors with powers to inspect and ultimately close premises
- Introduced criminal liabilities
- Established general duties for employers of more that five employees.

General duties under health and safety

Under the Act employers are required to

- Prepare a health and safety statement
- bring the statement to the attention of the workforce and notify them of changes
- the length and complexity of the statement will depend on the employer's business

Miscellaneous legislation

The following also contain provisions relating to health and safety.

- Management of Health & Safety at Work Regs. 1999
- Control of Substances Hazardous to Health Regs. 1999
- Fire Precautions Act, as amended for workplaces, 1999.

Regulations

Other matters covered by Regs. include:

- Accident reporting, including injuries, diseases and dangerous occurrences.
- Display screen equipment
- Electricity
- First aid
- Equipment use at work
- Risk assessment
- Manual handling
- Noise
- Workplace standards
- Safety representative in the workplace

Data Protection

The 1984 Data Protection Act was extended in 1998 to encompass the EU Data Protection Directive 1995. The key aims are to ensure:

- commons standards throughout the EU
- to enhance the protection of consumers and employers and giving them legal redress through the civil courts or by seeking the assistance of the Information Commissioner

Data is defined as:

- information being processed manually or by means of equipment or electronically

and also since 1998

- information held as part of a relevant filing system

This means that certain manual records and paper files are now covered.

Data Protection Principles

The principles require that personal data must:

- be processed fairly and lawfully
- be obtained only for specific, lawful purposes
- be adequate, relevant and not excessive
- be accurate and kept up to date
- not be kept longer than necessary
- be processed in accordance of the data subjects' rights
- protected against unlawful or unauthorised processing and accidental loss or damage.
- not be transferred outside the EU

Access and information

Employees must be allowed access to their personal record. They:

- must apply in writing to the Data Controller (nominated by the organisation)
- may be charged up to £10
- must be responded to promptly and in not more than 40 days
- have the right to have any inaccuracies withdrawn or corrected
- have the right to seek legal enforcement and remedies from the Information Commissioner and from the Information Tribunal.

Data exempted from access requests

The Data Controller will not have to comply with a request for access in respect of:

- data where a breach of confidence might arise
- references
- management data for forecasting and business and HR planning
- negotiations

Other legislation specific to data

- Medical records
- Criminal records
- Freedom of Information Act, 2000
- Regulations of Investigatory Powers Act, 2000

Monitoring of information sent by e-mail or phone is a complex area. Rights of employers to monitor, eg for training purposes are balanced by the Human Rights Act right to privacy.

Termination of employment

An employer has the right to terminate the employment of an employee provided that:

- full and proper notice is given, or pay in lieu of notice
- that the reason for the dismissal is fair and reasonable
- due process has been followed

Notice

- This must not be less than the statutory minimum > 1 month but< 1 year: 1 week> 2 years but < 12 years: 1 week for each year of service
- Failure to do so may result in claim for wrongful dismissal

Reason

Under the Employment Rights Act, 1996, fair reasons are:

- conduct
- capability
- redundancy
- statutory bar
- some other substantial reason (SOSR)

Due process

Normally applies to dismissal for misconduct:

- proper evidence is gathered.
- support, training etc offered if appropriate.
- allowing time for required improvement
- applying the appropriate stages and provisions of the agreed disciplinary procedure
- special rules apply for redundancy

Automatically unfair dismissals

Automatically unfair reasons

- trade union membership/ activities
- maternity related
- taking action on health and safety grounds
- seeking to exercise statutory employment protection rights
- refusing or opting out of Sunday working
- making a protected disclosure
- taking or seeking to take parental leave or adoption leave
- seeking to enforce rights under minimum wage
- seeking to enforce rights under the working time directive
- Transfer of undertaking, unless for economic, technological or organisational reason

Summary dismissal

This is dismissal without notice or pay in lieu of notice and must relate to an act of gross misconduct, eg fighting.

Nonetheless the correct **PROCESS** vis a vis the disciplinary procedure must be followed

Constructive dismissal

This is where an employee feels forced to resign due to the behaviour of the employer. The employee must show the employer's behaviour fundamentally breached the contract.

Disciplinary procedures

When dismissal takes place as a result of misconduct, the employer must show that due process was followed. Under the Employment Act 2002, the Statutory Dismissal and Disciplinary procedure must be followed.

- Standard procedure
  - Step 1 statement of grounds for action in writing and invitation to meeting
  - Step 2 meeting, discussion and decision
  - Step 3 appeal and appeal meeting
- Modified procedure (for summary dismissal)
  - Step 1 statement of grounds for dismissal in writing
  - Step 2 appeal and appeal meeting

Grievance procedures

Also under the Employment Act 2002, employees will only be able to claim unfair dismissal at an ET if the internal grievance procedure has been exhausted.

- Step 1 statement of grievance in writing
- Step 2 meeting, discussion, decision
- Step 3 appeal

Modified procedure for former employees

- Step 1 statement of grievance in writing
- Step 2 response in writing

Scrupulous, detailed and authenticated records must be kept of each and every stage of these procedures.

These statutory procedures will not come into force until October 2004.

8: Ethics and social responsibility

Topic List

- Boundary management
- The social and ethical environment
- Social responsibility
- Ethics in organisations

Business ethics is a topic of growing importance and companies are coming under increasing pressure to demonstrate their ethical credentials.

Business and society

Basic legal and economic theory assumes that the business exist to make a profit for its owners. This is too simple an approach for the complexity of modern society.

Stakeholder view

A business has other stakeholders besides its owners, in particular its employees and the community, who have particular interests in employment and negative externalities like pollution. The stakeholder view is that there should be a balance between the interests of the various stakeholder groups. It is the job of management to achieve this balance. NB ordinary financial accounting practice does not encourage such a balance, since it concentrates on costs, revenues and profit.

A variety of objectives - *Ansoff*

- **Primary economic objective** of optimising the firm's 'total resource-conversion process'
- **Non-economic social objectives** are **secondary** and balance the interests of stakeholder groups
- **Responsibilities** are undertaken but are not part of the mission (eg charitable donations)
- **Boundaries** restrict management's freedom of action (eg law, codes of conduct, trade union agreements)

A wide range of influences impinges on a business's behaviour. All are generally considered connected with ideas of right and wrong but they have dissimilar levels of authority

Law must be **obeyed** under pain of sanction against the organisation and individuals within it.

Custom, attitudes and belief vary between countries, regions, classes and persons. Businesses must be **sensitive**.

Ethics are concerned both with abstract concepts of **right and wrong** and with their practical application. Dishonesty, hypocrisy, aggression and exploitation will be frowned upon, if discovered.

Ethical dilemmas

Conflicting views of the organisation's responsibilities create ethical dilemmas for managers at all levels.

- Dealing with corrupt or unpleasant regimes
- Honesty in advertising
- Employees – cost or asset?
- Corrupt payments to officials – extortion, bribery or gift? The local culture must be considered.

Social responsibility of business is ill-defined in common usage but focuses on the provision of specific benefits to society beyond the scope of the organisation's commercial purpose. Examples include charitable donations, the preservation of employment and spending on environmental purposes.

For

- The law does not adequately protect those affected by business actions
- Business cannot exist without inputs from society such as economic infrastructure
- Capitalism is inherently exploitative and inequitable
- Shareholders are generally ineffective at controlling management

Against

- Legal respect for property rights mean that shareholder's ownership must not be abused
- Businesses benefit society by their economic activity: output and employment result
- Improper activity should be the business of law-makers not unrepresentative pressure groups
- Most large businesses are owned by institutional investors such as pension funds and insurance companies that provide widely available social benefits

Promoting and enforcing ethical behaviour

Professional ethics are laid down by professional bodies such as CIPD but apply to their members only.

Professional standards such as GAAP are influenced by professional bodies with corporate responsibility in mind and supported by.

Government leads the development of ethical behaviour by establishing best practice via **commissions** on standards. Some findings may become law.

Free flow of information to stakeholders tends to inhibit wrongdoing by senior managers.

Non-executive directors may remain objective and promote ethical behaviour (eg in senior manager remuneration).

Integrity based programmes promote ethical behaviour via leadership by management, ethics committees, ethics hotlines, a written code of behaviour and protection for **whistleblowers**.